David Cook

PATIENTS'
CHOICE

SPIRE

DEDICATION

To the Fellows, students and staff
of Green College, Oxford.

Spire is an imprint of Hodder & Stoughton *Publishers*

British Library Cataloguing in Publication Data

A catalogue record for this book is available from the British Library

ISBN 0-340-56899-2

*Printed in Great Britain for Hodder and Stoughton Limited, Mill Road, Dunton
Green, Sevenoaks, Kent by Clays Ltd, St. Ives plc.
Typeset by Phoenix Typesetting, Ilkley, West Yorkshire.*

Hodder and Stoughton Editorial Offices: 47 Bedford Square, London WC1B 3DP.

CONTENTS

INTRODUCTION

For the younger generation, their picture of doctors and hospitals comes from watching television programmes like *Casualty* and their own experience. The older among us were brought up on *Dr. Finlay's Case Book* and *Emergency Ward Ten*. As a society, our traditional understanding and experience of the medical world has been transformed from the cottage hospital and the caring, avuncular pillar of the community – the GP – to a world of health centres, high technology in hospitals and specialist doctors.

What has not changed, but is constantly under threat, is the basic relationship between doctors and patients. We take it for granted and are extremely glad it is there when we need it. But there are important trends in medical care which have affected and may change our attitudes to our doctors and their attitudes to us as patients.

This book is designed to lead us as patients through the complicated world of medicine from the local GP to the hospital doctor. It explains what we as patients can expect and are entitled to from our doctors and what they expect from us. Each chapter deals with a specific area of medical care. Perhaps you will not read the whole book at one sitting, but rather use it when you do have to go to the doctor. To help with this, each chapter is self-contained. Details which are important are repeated in the relevant chapters rather than requiring lots of turning to other sections. This book will tell you what the rights and responsibilities of patients and doctors are in our changing world. It will look at the doctor–patient relationship and the general themes of giving and getting consent, and confidentiality. It will explore the ethical and legal issues that face us as patients and as doctors in fertility; as parents and as children; as we have medical treatment and drugs prescribed for us; in decisions to accept, refuse, stop or withdraw treatment; and in caring for us in dying. As well as this we will be examining the issues of suicide, euthanasia, the wider roles of doctors, research, and the allocation of resources. Finally, we will try to put the specific guidelines and critical reflection on these issues in the context of the kind of ethical outlook which doctors have today.

This book is meant to be a practical, down-to-earth guide to provide us with the kinds of questions we should be asking of our doctors. It will deal in an honest way with the concerns which affect us as patients and our decisions about our treatment.

But before we leap into the detail of each area, we need to understand the context of medicine and medical ethics. Things make better sense if we know the forces and pressures at work shaping and moulding what happens in the area of health care.

For example

Suppose I suffer from amoebic dysentery. (It is a deeply moving experience.) So I visit the doctor. If the doctor listened to all my symptoms and then said, 'Well, I'm sorry. I hope you get better soon. Next patient please', then I would be pretty cross. We expect doctors to give us something for whatever we are suffering from. A good doctor often seems like the doctor who gives us what we want.

The danger in all this is that the doctor becomes nothing more or less than a need-meeter. We expect all our needs to be met. If I have a pain, if I need a baby, if I need to get rid of a baby, if I want a face-lift or to die with dignity, then for every one of these 'needs' we may be expecting doctors to supply solutions to all our dis-eases. Obviously, medicine and doctors cannot do everything. But there is a more important question. Are doctors only meant to meet patients' needs? Are all needs to be met regardless? Does a good doctor sometimes say 'No' to a patient? One helpful distinction doctors often used is between what a patient needs as opposed to what a patient wants. As patients, we must consider whether what we are asking for is what we want or is genuinely what we need. Even then, society and the doctor may still not judge our need to be so important that it is met, especially when there may be other people with other needs, which society thinks of as more important.

I work in a college where many people are teaching and studying medicine. People think it a bit odd for a philosopher and theologian to be based there. I tell them it is so that when I have my coronary,

I will be really well looked after. In the West, all of us expect that the wonders of high-technology medicine will do remarkable things for us. It certainly can do remarkable things. We can have a liver, kidney, heart and lung transplant. We can keep people alive on machines, when, only a few years ago, they would probably have died. We can help the infertile have babies and stop the fertile from having them with contraceptives ranging from an injection to the 'morning-after' Pill. We *can* do all of these things and much, much more, but *ought* we to do them? The rise and availability of new technologies and drugs raises hard questions about what we have the right to expect. Those expectations must be limited not just by morality or money, but by our concern for a world where many die because of a lack of basic health care.

The traditional picture of a doctor who knew best and was certainly not to be questioned, far less doubted, is breaking down. There has been a shift towards 'patient power'. Doctors themselves have often helped and encouraged this change in the way we see and relate to them. As patients we want to know more about what is happening to us, what options there are in treatment, what the results will be if we are treated and if we are not. We want to be totally and genuinely involved in our treatment. This puts new kinds of pressures on doctors. They are required not just to be good at medicine, but also at communicating, counselling and sharing decisions with us as patients.

This has also been happening as doctors increasingly work as members of interdisciplinary teams. Nurses, social workers, pharmacists, physical and occupational therapists, as well as doctors and a host of other professional groups are actively involved in our care. Doctors have had to learn to share responsibility for us with their other groups and to recognise that these folk have their own special expertise to share, which will benefit us as patients. This is not always easy, where doctors have been trained to make their own decisions and then find themselves having to explain and defend those decisions to other people and especially to patients. This shift has created a new atmosphere between patients and doctors. There is no hint that we are doing the doctor a favour by going to visit him or her. Rather, the doctor is there to make sure we are properly cared for when we are ill.

Medicine and the media

Doctors are more publicly answerable to us and to society. Newspapers, radio and television regularly question doctors and their representatives about their views, decisions and practices. The media is very quick to expose and condemn bad practices and this can make doctors uneasy about talking to reporters. Such public discussion does give patients the information they need to ask doctors about new diseases and treatments, and to have more detailed explanations of the treatments they receive.

None of us is above the law and the law affects doctors in two kinds of ways. As we shall see in what follows, the law of the land often controls and legislates what doctors are allowed and forbidden to do. Both social and civil law are relevant to many areas of medicine. That can mean that doctors practise medicine in a defensive way. The danger is that they may be defending themselves from court cases and being sued, rather than looking after us as patients in our best interests. This has not been the general attitude of doctors in the United Kingdom, but it is the case in the United States. It provides a useful warning to us all, that if we use law to organise and regulate what happens in medicine, we may lose the range and quality of care we have come to expect. We may also force the costs of medical care even higher, where insurance premiums for doctors become so high that medical costs escalate.

Law influences medicine in another way. The Abortion Law gave doctors permission to perform abortions under certain controlled conditions. That permission has now widened in practice, so the general public's expectation is for abortion on demand. Society expects doctors to be willing to provide abortions. Some feel that this created what amounts to a requirement on staff in obstetrics and gynaecological units to take part. The law is a blunt instrument and with laws covering abortion, fertility, surrogacy and proposals for living wills and for euthanasia under consideration, doctors are seeing their clinical freedom and judgement affected by the law of the land. This might mean that doctors are more responsible to society as a whole. It also might make the practice of medicine quite different, as what is legal becomes more important than what is morally right or in the best interests of patients.

The British Medical Association

Much of the work for this book was done while the author was a member of the BMA Medical Ethics Handbook Working Party. The detailed evidence and discussions showed a remarkable willingness on the part of the medical community to set out the moral basis for the work they do. The results of that working party will be published in 1993 as *Medical Ethics Today: its practice and philosophy*. This publication will make a major contribution to medical ethics and be the guide for doctors in the United Kingdom. What the new book does is to take a 'snapshot' of the state of medical ethics and to describe how doctors see developments in many key areas of medicine and morality. *Medical Ethics Today* sets down how doctors are to behave from the viewpoint of the medical profession. I thought it seemed only fair that a parallel book was produced written from the patient's point of view. *Patients' Choice* will offer a different perspective on issues of medical ethics today.

Books do not come from nothing. Many years of contact with doctors and patients in various medical schools have given a tremendous amount of insight as well as information. But books only get written because of encouragement, support and hard work. James Catford of Hodder and Stoughton and Katie Wasson, my researcher at the Whitefield Institute, have both worked extremely hard to make the book possible and see it produced on time. I also want to thank Sue Elston and Kathleen Cook for helping with the typing and Simon and Kenneth, my sons, for proof-reading and helping with indexing the book. I am grateful to them all.

Beyond all of this there has been a rise in the importance of medical ethics. There is a clear difference between what is legal and what is moral or ethical. This book is more concerned about areas of medical ethics – the rights and wrongs of medical behaviour – rather than just what is legal in the practice of medicine, though that will be referred to as we examine each issue. Doctors are usually seen as being conservative in society and that is genuinely true. But doctors are people too and live, as we all do, in a multi-cultural, multi-faith, pluralistic society, where there are many competing moral beliefs, attitudes and practices. Where there is such variety, it is all the more important that we all know what doctors think about the moral questions in medicine and what kinds of discussion and level of agreement there are among medical people on contentious issues. This book attempts to provide that information, stressing how that affects patients.

One further factor affects the practice and philosophy of medicine in our society and that factor is the Government. The radical changes in the National Health Service, with greater stress on patient choice and efficiency, are having a dramatic effect on what is happening at every level of medical care. We need to bear this in mind as we look at the specific issues that face us. It also reminds us that the practice and philosophy of medicine is dynamic, not static. Things are changing all the time, with new discoveries, reactions, laws and debates in medical matters. What we write and read today will be like a snapshot of where we have reached in medicine. Much will change, but even in the midst of these changes the basic values and moral standards remain the same. We shall refer to these throughout the book and return to them in the final chapter. In the meantime, our task is to explore medical ethics in a very practical way, and that means beginning with patient choice and the doctor–patient relationship.

Patient questions

To make the right choices as a patient it is essential that you ask the right questions. To help you do this, questions have been listed at the end of each chapter which need to be asked either of your doctor or yourself. They are given only as a guide, but they should enable you to make the most of short consultation times with health care professionals as well as to evaluate your own attitude towards your medical situation.

1

CHOICE AND CONSENT

Before we can be clear what it means for a patient to give or refuse to give consent to medical treatment, we must understand the doctor–patient relationship. There are three basic models that seem to operate in our society. The first is the old-fashioned *paternalistic relationship*. It rests on the view that the doctor knows best. The patient is at the mercy of the doctor, who may or may not decide to tell the patient what is happening and why it is being done. This approach did not encourage patients to ask questions, but rather to leave everything about care and treatment to the doctor. The advantage was that each of us handed over all responsibility to the doctor and did not have to worry about what happened, as long as the doctor really did know best. Times have changed and we have all come to see that medicine deals with our own bodies. Because they belong to us we should have the major say in what happens to them and to us. We have also had to recognise that doctors do not know everything and do not always make proper judgements about what is best for us.

So there is a second type of relationship, which we can call the *consumer model*. In this relationship the patient is the consumer and the doctor is providing a medical service. It is up to the patient to choose which doctor and which service he or she wants. Recent Health Department publications have stressed the importance of maximising patient choice. The consumer model puts our choice as patients at the centre. The problem is that we may not be in the best position to choose because we do not really know what is best for us. That is why we have gone to see a doctor in the first place. We need his or her help. At the same time, the consumer relationship reduces the role of the doctor to a mere need-meeter or service provider. Given all the training, experience and expertise of doctors, there seems to be more to being a doctor than just responding to our demands.

Doctors and Patients in a Partnership

The best model for doctors and patients is one of partnership. In this relationship, the doctor is the medical expert with skill and training and a willingness to do what is best for us, both in treatment and advice. The patient goes to the doctor for help. He or she is suffering dis-ease and perhaps from a disease. What we as patients need is help to understand what is wrong with us, what can be done about it, what different treatments we might have, which of these is best for us as individuals, what will happen if we have or do not have the treatment, and how we should look after ourselves and our health.

For the doctor to do his or her job properly, patients have to be frank and honest. There is no point in pretending or covering up things which the doctor needs to know to help us. Withholding such information might mean that the wrong treatment is given and we could end up worse off than we began. Patients not only need to give doctors all the information they need to do the job properly, they also need to do what the doctor tells them. Of course, the doctor must explain to us what is wrong, what treatment is recommended, and why we are being given the medicine or care we are given. But patients must take their medicine, keep the doctor informed as to what is happening to them, and complete the course of treatment.

Both partners have vital roles to play. Obviously, doctors will know far more about illness, disease, treatment and cures than patients, but patients know far more about their own bodies, circumstances, fears, worries and wants than anyone else. Together patients and doctors can overcome the problem of ill health and disease.

Doctors must therefore listen to patients to understand their circumstances and needs as well as their physical or mental problems. Doctors also need to be aware that patients want and need different amounts of information at different times. Patients must have information presented to them in a way they can understand and grasp. There is now much more training for doctors on how to listen and communicate better with patients. A good doctor will ask what the patient wants to know and then give what is wanted in a clear and understandable way. Patients must realise that what is important to us may not be as important to a doctor. A woman who is being offered a mastectomy (removal of a breast) may be more worried about how she will look and feel than about the risk of recurring cancer. The medical expert needs to have a genuinely human touch to give patients confidence not just in medical skill and knowledge, but in the doctor's commitment to the best interests of the patient.

Limits to this Partnership

Doctors are responsible to us as individual patients, but they are usually employed by the National Health Service and have many other patients as well as us. Doctors are responsible to society in general. When they treat us as patients, they must also be aware of their responsibility to other people, especially if these other people's health may be at risk from us and from the treatment we receive. There are limited resources and treatments available. The question of how to allocate our scarce health resources will be examined later in the chapter, but we must not imagine that doctors can or will give us whatever we want.

In a way, doctors act as gate-keepers to treatments. They control who will get treatment and what treatment they will have. To give one patient an expensive treatment or drug means that other patients may not get what they need. Only the doctor is in a position to decide. We may agree to a treatment, want it and even demand it, but a doctor is not obliged to give us the drug or treatment we want. It may be too expensive. There may also be cheaper and equally successful alternatives available.

Some patients, like Jehovah's Witnesses, have particular religious beliefs which forbid them to use blood or blood products. Doctors should try as far as possible to accommodate these beliefs, but may have to explain to the patient the limits all of us face in having alternative treatments. Some patients may want doctors to give them drugs or treatments which doctors believe are bad for patients. People who want help with slimming may ask for drugs to suppress their appetites, without realising that such drugs can harm the body. Even when we know that drugs do harm the body we may still ask for them. Weightlifters and athletes often look for steroids to help build up their bodies and to enhance their performances. Where doctors are convinced that such drugs are harmful, they cannot be required to give them to patients. Patients cannot ask a doctor to give a treatment or drug which is harmful, even though they might be willing to accept the risks of harm in return for benefit gained.

Doctors have to be free to use their medical skill and knowledge and to act in ways which satisfy moral, legal and practical standards. When we face a doctor in the consulting room or hospital, that doctor ought to be concerned for each of us as individuals, but there is also a wider responsibility to society and to what is best for us. We shall see in the Chapter on Choice and Confidentiality that a doctor might have a duty to breach the partnership with an individual patient if someone else's life and well-being are in danger. Partnerships between doctors and patients are limited.

Partnerships have a beginning, and one key element in patient choice is choosing our own doctor. General Practitioners are obliged to have some kind of practice leaflet describing what they offer and provide as services to their patients. Ideally, such leaflets should also tell us the philosophy and outlook of the doctors in the practice and what values they uphold. Information about services and values help us as patients decide with which doctor and practice we should register. Our choice at the hospital level is much more restricted. Here the GP usually refers us to a particular clinic, or we may attend an Accident and Emergency Unit and be seen by whoever is on duty, who then sends us on to the medical team and unit relevant to our need. GPs have a responsibility to send their patients to the best specialists they know and to do so they need to have regular links and contact with hospitals and their medical teams.

A patient may decide to change doctors for various reasons. Moving district is the most common reason for changing our doctors, but we might be unhappy with the services provided or the values of the practice. We have the right and the freedom to change doctors, so entering into a partnership also means that we can leave that relationship and begin a fresh one.

Doctors are people too, and what is sauce for the goose is sauce for the gander. Some doctors, both in hospital and general practice, are faced with violence and abuse by their patients. Such patients cannot be left untreated, especially in emergency situations. Hopefully, doctors can persuade other colleagues to deal with the difficult patient. If that fails, they may call in a counsellor, try gaining help from family and friends, or in desperation treat the patient in a secure, separate area from other patients, with some kind of support in attendance. General Practitioners can request that a patient be removed from their list. This can only take place when a patient is not actually receiving a particular treatment. The Family Health Services Authority is responsible for helping the patient find another doctor. If the patient abuses or is violent to all doctors, then the local Family Health Services Authority will arrange a rota system. In extreme circumstances a doctor may have to have a police officer on hand to provide protection.

Doctors, like patients, have the freedom to refuse to enter into a partnership or to bring it to an end. But that medical freedom is restricted in emergency situations. Patients must be treated if their life is at risk. Doctors also have a responsibility to make sure that further treatment is provided for a patient, if he or she is unwilling to carry on treating the patient. This might arise where a doctor has a strong moral objection to abortion. Even if the doctor believes that abortion is wrong and refuses to have anything to do with signing an abortion form, doctors are required to send the patient on to another doctor, who would be willing to look at the situation again and would, in principle, be willing to provide an abortion, if it is legally or medically required.

If doctors work in very isolated communities, their freedom of choice, like the patient's, will be restricted in practice. It may not be realistic to find another doctor, even if both the patient and the doctor would prefer that situation. In such circumstances, the doctor must continue to care for and treat the patient.

In consenting to a partnership, doctors and patients can also refuse to accept each other. There are some important limits to the doctor–patient relationship.

Insurance and Employment Medicals

Sometimes we have to have a medical for a new job, for an insurance policy, or if we are going to live and work abroad. Then we have no choice in which doctor we see. We cannot give or refuse consent in these settings. But that fact does not mean that the doctor has no responsibility towards us even if we are not really his or her patient, except for a very short time.

We as patients have the right to know what will happen to the information we provide to doctors in such an examination. We also have the right to know what will happen to whatever is observed about our health. Such information is not usually being collected for the patient's good or health, but for the purposes of employment or to assess insurance risks. The doctor must explain what he is doing and why, and who will be given the information. What information will be passed on must also be clear. We, as patients, may decide not to give all the information we might to a doctor in these circumstances. If we do that, we need to remember that the doctor can only report on the information he or she has. If we omit some crucial fact, it may make a difference later on.

This is less of a problem if it is our own GP who is examining us for the medical. We are entitled to see his or her report according to the Access to Medical Reports Act 1988. We patients need to be careful here. Sometimes we sign forms for a job or insurance policy stating that we are happy for the company to contact our GP. This agreement means that the doctor may tell the company anything on our medical record. A good doctor should check with us before revealing anything that might be damaging to our application, but patients must not leave all the responsibility to the GP. We have the right and the responsibility to see what is written about us by our own doctor. We should make sure we do check what is said about us and that we are happy with it.

When the doctor is not our own, but employed by the company to give us a medical, we have no right to see the report written about us. We do however have the right to know if there is something wrong with us which is important. However, we will not be told directly. Medical etiquette usually works by doctors talking to other doctors. If an examining doctor finds something wrong with us, he or she should contact and inform our GP or the Chief Medical Officer of the area in which we live, and it is then their responsibility to follow the matter up with us.

Giving and Getting Consent

When we talk about giving or getting consent, we do not just mean signing a consent form. Consent may be expressed and withdrawn in a formal manner, or given not just by what we say but also by what we do. Explicit consent is usually given by verbal or written agreement. Implicit consent is where we go to consult the doctor, tell him or her about what is wrong with us, or even roll up our sleeve or unbutton our blouse to allow examination, blood pressure to be measured, or heart sounds to be heard with a stethoscope. Obviously, our consent only covers specific examinations or treatment done at that point and nothing else.

But why does consent matter so much? Sadly, some doctors seem to think that getting consent is a way of defending themselves against a legal case. If a doctor does not gain proper consent, then he or she may be liable to a charge of battery or negligence. We shall look at the exact legal situation later in this chapter. This is a very defensive view on the part of doctors. If there is a sense of partnership, then consent is much more a matter of respect for the other person and making sure their rights are protected.

Patient choice means that we patients are free to decide what happens to our own bodies. This rests on the high view of the value, worth and dignity of each individual person. To make decisions about what happens to us as patients requires full, understandable and proper information from the doctor. For our consent to be valid, we must be fully informed, able to make a proper decision, and free from any wrong kind of pressure or force. Patient self-determination is at the heart of giving and getting consent.

There is also a very practical reason for a doctor getting the consent of a patient. Such a person is much more likely to act in ways which will help and not hinder the treatment given. If we give our consent, we are better prepared for what will happen to us. If we know that the doctor has told us all that might happen to us and explained as fully as possible what is wrong, how we will be treated and the possible consequences and reactions to that treatment, then we will not worry. Doctors know that patients do worry, but if we are told what is going on, then we can relax and that maximises our chances of getting better more quickly.

Patients must play their part

Medicine is an art and not just a science. It cannot do everything and is not always successful. Some doctors are unwilling to tell patients when they do not know what will happen or to be honest when talking of the limits of medical science. As patients we have a choice. We can know all the facts and the limits of what medicine can and cannot do. Or we can instead make it clear that we would rather not know all the things that might go wrong and all the nasty things that might happen. There is a fine line here, where doctors very properly are concerned about the best interests of the patient. Doctors might feel that some of us would worry too much and that would do us harm as well as restrict our recovery. It is important that we as patients make it clear to the doctor how much we do and do not want to know. Doctors are not mind-readers. Patients must help doctors to know how much to tell us. That decision may mean knowing everything, or enough to have confidence that the doctors will do their best.

When we are patients, we may not want to make decisions. We are ill, sometimes in a strange world of odd smells, vocabulary and ways of behaving. We may want the doctors and nurses to take responsibility for us and to make our decisions for us. As patients we can choose to let the doctor make decisions for us. That choice must be a genuine option for us as patients and the doctor has the privileged role of then making these choices. If we feel that the doctor does know best and will only do what is in our best interests, then the choice may be given over to the doctor. That decision does not mean that we lose all responsibility. We are still responsible for our choice to let the doctor choose and will have to be offered other choices as the treatment and its results continue.

Doctors are placed in a very difficult position because they not only have to be able to give us the information we need about what is wrong with us and what can be done about it in language we can grasp, but they must also decide how much we want to know, can take and are asking about our case. Doctors ought not to force information, or doubt and uncertainties on us as patients, especially if we are feeling vulnerable and unable to cope. Doctors need to be sensitive to us and to what we want to know and how we will respond to that knowledge. As patients, we have to help doctors to make these judgements about how much information and detail we should be given. What we say directly and the questions we ask and don't ask will guide the doctor. We must make it clear when we do not want to know any more. That is our role. The doctor should tell us everything that is important about our problem and its treatment, unless we obviously do not want to have all the gory details.

Signing a Consent Form

In the past, the signing of a consent form was to protect doctors from the charge of assault. While there remains a hangover of this view, seeking consent now has a much more positive role. When we as patients co-operate willingly in a treatment, that treatment is more likely to be successful. If a patient believes that a treatment will work, then, for many of us, it does. If no consent is given, then the doctor may have a hard time giving us the treatment and the results may not be very good. Of course, the signing of a consent form does provide a kind of defence against any criminal charges of battery or assault or even a civil action for damages because of trespass done to a person.[1]

♣ *Consent is a process not an event.* In this way the signing of a form is proof that a process of explanation and agreement took place, not the actual process itself. It is far more important that we as patients were given the information we required than that we put our names on a piece of paper.

As we can give consent, so we can refuse treatment. If we want to refuse a particular treatment or to leave hospital against the advice of a doctor, then we will be asked to sign a form which states that we accept responsibility for what we are doing, we understand the likely consequences of our actions and refusal, and that these consequences have been explained to us.

Giving consent is not a once-for-all event. The giving and getting of consent is a process that continues and changes as a treatment proceeds and the results of that treatment are felt. Once we have given consent, then doctors will assume that we are still consenting unless and until we change our minds and tell the doctor of that change. It is our responsibility as patients to inform doctors of any change in what we want done to us. Some women may want to have as 'natural' a childbirth as possible but, in the midst of labour, the woman might change her mind and want some drugs or other kind of help. Doctors must be ready to adapt to what the patient wants, if at all possible.

A patient's consent is always given for a particular purpose. Such consent covers particular treatments, drugs or operations. A doctor is not entitled to go beyond what has been discussed and agreed. A doctor ought not to do more in an operation than was agreed, unless there is an emergency situation and it is not possible to gain our consent as a patient. A woman who is undergoing an operation for a blocked fallopian tube, ought not to wake up to find that a hysterectomy has been performed. Consent must be gained for any major step which goes beyond the specific consent given. Only in a matter of life and death is a doctor justified in acting in any way above and beyond what has been consented to and agreed.

Fully Informed Consent

The standard set for doctors in dealing with us as patients is very high and rightly so. When consent is discussed in medical settings, the most common phrase used is 'fully informed valid consent'. It stresses two different aspects of consent. To give our consent we need to have all the appropriate information and we must also be free from force or pressure to decide one way or the other.

The good doctor is a good communicator. That means giving information in a way which we patients can understand and where there is enough time for it to sink in and for us to digest and respond to that information. Medical schools are increasing the emphasis on teaching students how to communicate more effectively. Good communication should be available for all patients, but is especially important if English is not the first language of a patient. It may not be possible to have an interpreter available and so doctors tend to rely on family or friends who are proficient in English. This runs the risk that the patient's wishes may not be accurately expressed, so there may be no genuine consent or refusal.

When a patient is seeking political asylum after being tortured in a particular country, it is less than ideal if interpreters from the embassy or diplomatic corps of that same country are used. The Medical Foundation for Care of Victims of Torture has expressed its concern over this danger. Doctors need to be aware that the information given through an interpreter, who could be biased, may have serious consequences for the patient and his or her family.

Fortunately, such cases are rare. The World Medical Association Declaration of Lisbon, 1981, states that doctors have a responsibility to make sure that their patients have enough information to make a proper decision. But how much is enough? This should be the amount of information we patients want and need to make up our minds. Legally speaking, enough is defined by how much information other doctors would give. In a very famous case, Lord Scarman described how much information should be given to a patient.[2] He began by stressing that the starting point was the right of the patient to make his or her own decision to accept or refuse any proposed treatment and the right to know about any significant risk involved.

The doctor must inform patients of serious risks involved in the treatment, unless it is obvious that giving the information about risk would harm the physical or mental health of the patient. The way to judge what counts as a significant risk is by asking if the patient would think it significant if told of the risk. To try to define that more exactly, Scarman suggested doctors ask what a reasonably prudent patient would think was significant in this situation. That seems to cover not just risks in general, but any particular risk which might be important to a patient. I was offered an operation on my palate to overcome a breathing and sleeping problem. There was no absolute guarantee of success and one of the risks was of a possible change to my voice. As someone who broadcasts fairly regularly, that risk was too high, so I declined the operation and looked for alternative treatments. Doctors must explain the risks and benefits not just of the proposed treatment but also of alternatives and if there were to be no treatment at all.

We need information to make proper choices. But choice is not just a matter of rationality. Our feelings, attitudes and values are part of our decision-making process. Doctors must be sensitive to us as people; how much we can take in and what we can cope with at any one time. We as patients should be in charge of how much information is given and when it is given.

Valid Consent

When we talk about valid consent, we mean consent that is genuinely our own, voluntarily given and free from pressure or force. We should examine some situations where there are particular dangers of such pressure, as in prisons or military services. But all of us can feel under pressure simply from the doctor and the medical setting. Patients 'allow' doctors to do all kinds of things because they are doctors and we find it very hard to say 'No' to them.

Being in hospital or living in an institution like a children's home or nursing home for the elderly can pressurise us to conform to what the institution wants and find easiest to cope with. Doctors need to be aware of such pressures on the young and the old, especially if people wish to send them to hospital or treat them with drugs in order to make them more amenable.

Families, too, can pressurise their members, especially where there are religious beliefs involved. Issues like abortion and blood transfusions provide cause for concern. Patients should have independent counselling and help. We should be encouraged to make our own decisions and not simply to reflect and fit in with what the family wants. Sociological evidence suggests that working-class people are more likely to agree to whatever doctors want in an almost automatic way. People from the middle classes, especially so-called intellectuals, are much more likely to disagree with what a doctor proposes and refuse to give consent.[3]

Teaching Settings

Many of our hospitals are teaching centres, where students learn by practising. When we are in hospital patients need to know when students are present and involved in treating us. We are free to ask to be seen without students being present. Consent must be obtained not just for students to be there but for any specific examination or treatment which a student might perform. Patient choice is crucial and must be respected.

To train students, doctors and nurses, a video or tape of a consultation may be made and used in teaching. This should not be done without our consent as a patient. We must be free to refuse to be taped. The fact of being taped might itself affect what happens between the doctor and us. Raising the issue requires sensitivity on the doctor's part to make sure that we will not be affected either by withholding vital information which might be embarrassing or feel forced to let the taping happen, when not really happy with the whole business. We need to know who will use, see or hear the tapes and how long that will continue. As communication links develop between various parts of the country, there may be very wide use made of such teaching aids.

In some Accident and Emergency Units, the resuscitation of patients is videoed and used both for teaching and assessment. The patient's face should be obscured unless he or she gives specific consent for the video's use, when they recover. If a doctor wishes to take photographs for teaching purposes or to illustrate research, then a patient must be told of the purpose. If there is a change of that purpose, then, where a patient might be identified, it is important to gain the patient's consent for the new purpose and use. Children and those who are unable to decide for themselves should only be recorded by photograph or video with the consent of the parents or those who care for them. Obviously, in abuse cases different rules apply. When a child is old enough to make a decision for himself or herself, then he or she is able to withdraw the permission for use of the visual material. The same applies to those who may regain the capacity to make decisions.

Research and Consent

We shall look at all the issues raised by research conducted by doctors in the Chapter on Research. In all research the issue of consent is vital. Patients are free to decide whether or not to take part in any research. So we need to know that there is a research project going on. We need to be specifically invited to take part in that research as a patient. We need to know the purpose and aim of the research, why it is necessary and what it hopes to discover, test or prove. We need to know the risks to us if we do not take part, as well as the likely benefits which might result. Obviously, if doctors already knew all the answers to these questions, there would be no need for research at all. It is because medicine does not have all the answers that we are being encouraged to take part in research activity.

The test of being fully informed and having a genuine choice is vital. There must be no pressure to take part or any hint that we are letting the doctor down or might not get good care if we do not help in this way. There may be direct benefits to us or to other people. Knowing that may make a difference to what we decide. We are not to be researched on without our explicit permission and that should be given in writing. The form should note that we have had all the relevant information given to us.

Research is controlled by local research committees and we as patients are free to see the descriptions (protocols) of the research project which have been submitted by the researchers and approved by the research committee. We are still free to take part or to refuse any part in that research.

HIV in the community

One area where consent is not being sought is in research to ascertain how widely HIV has spread in the heterosexual community. There is a major epidemiological study to ascertain the pattern of incidence and spread of HIV. This involves the testing of blood of pregnant women going to hospital. They may not be clearly informed that this test is taking place and not asked for their consent.

Such testing looks like a direct contradiction to all that is normal practice. The difference here is that the HIV testing is anonymous and not for the benefit of the patient or the doctor. It is a piece of research to see how a disease is spreading. The results are not given to patients or to doctors. In that sense, it is not like a normal HIV test, where a patient asks for the test, is counselled about the implications of being tested and having a positive result, and then given the test results. As patients, we have the right to know that such epidemiological, anonymous testing is happening. Most of us will be glad that government and medical researchers are trying to find out exact information about HIV and AIDS and will be delighted to help, especially as there will be no direct result for individual patients. Others may feel uneasy about taking a test which is not for their direct benefit and where the information gained could be very important. If I were HIV positive, I would want to know about it. Any doctors treating me would also want and need to know that I was HIV positive, as they might be at risk. We have not been able to devise a way of testing large groups of people in society to learn about the spread of diseases, whilst at the same time maintaining confidentiality, obtaining fully informed, valid consent and protecting the anonymity and well-being of the patient.

Prisoners, the Armed Services and Consent

If someone is in prison or on remand, then he or she has lost not just their freedom but also some of the rights the rest of society enjoys. However, the basic freedom to choose in relation to medical procedures still remains. Obviously, as patients in prison we may not be free to choose which doctor we want to consult. The prison doctor, however, is still responsible for making sure that prisoners do give proper consent to medical treatment. In a situation where there is little privacy and there may be a good deal of pressure to conform from those in authority, doctors have an even greater responsibility to protect the interests of prison patients.

The prison authorities may want to conduct an intimate body search for drugs, but the prisoner should still give consent for that examination. That consent may be overridden if there is danger of a crime being committed or if there is a risk to other people. Ideally, prison patients should give consent for such searches and for the compulsory medical examination when they enter prison. None of us is above the law and that may require a prisoner's refusal to give consent to be overridden in the interests of others.

As prisoners lose some of their freedoms, so those who enter the armed forces are not as free as the rest of us. Part of belonging to the Forces is to accept these limits and to be under pressure in areas of consent and confidentiality. Orders must be obeyed, but these should not conflict with the genuine consent of a member of the Forces without any undue pressure from those in authority. The doctor, even if a member of the Forces and under orders, must act as the advocate of the patient in the Forces and protect his or her rights and freedom to choose.

Refusing Treatment

In describing the process of giving and getting consent, we have stressed that patients can accept or reject treatment. That basic freedom of patients is legally expressed in the famous case *Sidaway* v. *the Board of Governors of the Bethlem Royal Hospital and the Maudsley Hospital* (*see* Note 2). Patients are free to refuse treatment for any reason, good or bad, and even for no reason at all. Obviously, doctors will want to know why we are refusing treatment and should tell us the risks of that refusal, what else can be done, and clear up any misunderstandings we may have. We may need more time to think again, but must not be pressurised into giving our consent. Doctors are not entitled to withdraw their support when we do not conform to their recommendations. In a partnership there may be disagreements, but the relationship continues and in that the doctor is still responsible for doing the best possible in light of our decision.

Some legal authorities suggest that refusing treatment, especially if there is a serious risk to our life or health, requires greater understanding on our part than simply giving consent. The more serious the implication and results, the more certain we need to be that this is a risk we accept and the more sure the doctor must be that we really understand and genuinely want what we have decided to do.[4]

Jehovah's Witnesses refuse to have blood transfusions. Doctors may be faced with a clear and consistent refusal to have a necessary, life-saving transfusion, and in such circumstances the doctor has a choice. He or she may accept the decision, recognising that the patient is a rational adult who is able to make up his own mind and would rather die than have a treatment which he regards as morally wrong. The alternative is to assume that the patient is not rational and that it is not in the patient's best interests to refuse treatment. This means that a doctor would not just consult his professional body, the British Medical Association and the Medical Defence Union or its equivalent, but also seek a court ruling to 'force' the patient to be treated. In cases where there is little doubt that a patient is rational, and even in cases where there may be some doubt, the law of the land generally favours the freedom of the patient to make a choice and in particular to refuse treatment if they so wish.⁵

The individual patient has the freedom to make up his or her own mind. Accepting or refusing treatment is our choice. To refuse treatment must be accepted by doctors. Our wishes as patients must be respected even if the doctor disagrees with them and knows them to be dangerous. As long as we understand what we are doing and the consequences, doctors must respect that decision.

When we cannot give Consent

Throughout this chapter, we have assumed that patients are fit and able to make their own decisions about treatment in partnership with their doctors. What happens when patients are not able to make such a decision or when they might never be able to decide?

In an Emergency

Patients are sometimes taken to hospital or to the doctor in an emergency. There is no way that consent can be given or refused. Urgent cases need immediate treatment. Patients may be unconscious or in deep trauma and shock as a result of an accident, heart attack or stroke. Patients must be treated and doctors have a legal as well as a moral responsibility to do whatever is necessary to save our lives. Doctors are only entitled to act in such emergencies if there is a genuine and serious risk to our health or to life itself. They cannot do anything and everything they might want to do. The aim must be to restore the patient, so each of us is able to make decisions about long-term health and care. Rules in emergencies only cover the emergency situation and not ordinary treatments.

Doctors are entitled to assume that we as patients would want to have our lives saved and our health safeguarded in an emergency. However, we might not want doctors to resuscitate us or to preserve our lives in certain circumstances, as when we have had a severe stroke. In such cases, we as patients might have completed a living will or advance directive which states what we wish and what we do not want a doctor to do. Of course, the doctor may not find this directive in an emergency and so common sense and the law would support life-saving measures. If our wishes are clear and the doctor is sure that we really understood what was going to happen and made a decision in the light of that knowledge, then the doctor must respect our wishes, as in the case of Jehovah's Witnesses.

More people are following the example of what happens in the United States and producing their own living wills or advance directives. This is a way of indicating what a patient wants to happen if a situation arises where communication and consent are impossible. This is part of a patient's choice. It is simply a written way of expressing what we as patients want in terms of accepting or rejecting various treatments. Some people are fearful of doctors doing too much and striving too hard to keep them alive, so as they grow older or perhaps face a situation where they might lose their mental capacities, as in senile dementia or Alzheimer's disease, they might draw up such a document.

These 'living wills' have no legal standing at the moment. They are expressions of what the patient would like and should be taken very seriously by doctors. If the doctor is certain that this has been properly considered and that the circumstances and situation were correctly understood, then the patient's wishes should be followed. If there is any doubt, then the bias is in favour of preserving life. While we as patients may make it clear that we do not want to have any 'burdensome' treatment, we are not entitled to pressurise a doctor to end our lives. This will be further explained in the Chapter on Suicide and Euthanasia.

In the United States and in Scotland, there is a way that someone else can act on our behalf when we are unable to decide for ourselves. It is quite clear that no one can give or refuse consent for what happens to an adult. However, the use of a 'proxy' in the US or a 'tutor dative' in Scotland can provide an expression of what patients want even though we are unable to speak for ourselves. These are not legally binding or even common in England, Northern Ireland or Wales, but there is increasing pressure to allow the use of a third party to have a a part in making decisions about our treatment when we are incapacitated, incompetent and unable to decide for ourselves.

Competent to Consent

Our decisions can be affected by all kinds of things. Alcohol, drugs, tiredness, fear and pain can all make a difference to our process of decision-making and its results. Sometimes, we may suffer from mental illness, or a disorder, which may be temporary or long term. This does not mean that we are unable to give consent. Different people have different abilities at different times in decision-making. When and how we are asked the question of consent may make a big difference to how much we can understand and how appropriately we may respond.

The assumption is that doctors will do what is best for us and that normally we are all happy to have treatment which is good for us and our health. To give consent need not mean understanding every little detail of the disease and its treatment but knowing that the treatment we have will help us get better. Our mental disorders or limitations do not excuse doctors from the responsibility of explaining what is happening to us and why.

In order to refuse treatment, doctors usually require that patients have a greater ability to understand what has been chosen and its consequences. They assume that most of us want to get well and have our diseases and illnesses treated. Because there may be doubt about our mental capacity to make appropriate decisions for ourselves, doctors are entitled to act in our best interests. This should be checked by other doctors and the nursing staff, who must act as the patient's advocate in settings where patients are unable to decide for themselves. The British Medical Association have produced 'Guidelines in Medical Treatment for Incapacitated Adults'.

Families have a key part to play in these situations. But families have no power or right to decide what happens to us as adults. Each of us alone is able to give or withhold consent. Families cannot make our decisions for us or on our behalf. Naturally, families can and do give doctors a clear picture of what we might want in certain circumstances. They provide a great deal of help in enabling medical staff to understand who we are and what we might have wished to happen to us in a life-threatening situation. Just because the families say that we would not want to live like this – for example, as a severely handicapped person after an accident – does not mean that it would have been our direct wish. Families may have their own axe to grind and wish to do us harm, as well as be genuinely concerned for our best interests. The doctor cannot and must not act simply on the basis of what the family and friends tell about us and our wishes. The best interests of the patient must be decided on medical grounds.

Children and Young People

Families, parents and guardians are in a position to give or withhold consent for children until they are old enough to make their own decisions. Exactly when that time comes will be discussed in the Chapter on Choice and Children. There has been an increasing shift in medicine to try to involve children more and more in decisions about what treatments they should have. As our children grow and mature, they take increasing responsibility for themselves and are able to make more decisions for themselves. Part of good parenting is learning to let children make their own choices, recognising that they will make mistakes and hopefully learn from them. Society, in general, has encouraged this process, particularly through the Children Act of 1989. It is always a good idea to involve children in decisions about what will happen to them. Now there is a move to making this a legal responsibility to ensure that it takes place, especially if a child has enough understanding and the ability to grasp what is going on.

If a child or young person is able to understand what is involved in taking or refusing a treatment, then their decision is sufficient to allow that treatment to proceed. This seems to limit the rights of parents and in situations of conflict doctors will and should do what the child wants, even if the parents are unhappy with that. The crucial factor is the level of competence of the child and this is explored in the Chapter on Choice and Children. However, if the child wishes to refuse treatment the law courts have drawn a distinction between being able to give consent and being able to refuse treatment. Children and their parents can give consent for treatment to happen. If parents try to refuse to allow a child any necessary and life-saving treatment, then they might be charged with neglect and the child made a ward of court to allow the treatment to take place. It seems that children are able to consent to a treatment, but there is more doubt as to whether a child can refuse to be treated, especially in a life-threatening situation.[6]

Difficult Issues in Consent

Normally, medical treatment is given because it is for the benefit of the patient and in his or her best interests. There are a number of situations which arise because of new technology and the need to train doctors in specific medical techniques.

Practising Intubation

When we have breathing problems, doctors may put in a tube to help us breathe more easily. This is called intubation. If this was going to happen to us, we would all prefer that doctors knew what they were doing and were experienced at doing it. How do doctors learn this technique? They might learn by practising on us, when we are in that situation. Alternatively, they might practise on newly dead people. While that may seem offensive to many folk in society, the reality is that in some Accident and Emergency Units, junior doctors do practise intubation on those who have just died. This is usually done without consent. The dead person cannot give consent and there is no time and no enthusiasm to intrude into the shock and distress of relatives.

Patients have the right to know that this is happening. It should not be done secretly, but should be part of a controlled education programme and ensure as much respect for the dead person as possible. Some feel that practising on dead people is not really a very useful guide to dealing with live people. They also think that living patients would be happy to consent to such practising of intubation if they needed to have the procedure anyway.

Even more upsetting is the knowledge that emergency resuscitation is also learned by practising on babies who have died. Parents are not consulted, because it is a very difficult time for them. If we had a sick baby who needed help to breathe, we would all prefer a doctor who was experienced and was good at resuscitating and intubation.

The problem is that to gain that expertise requires practice and the easiest way to learn is by practising on newly dead babies.

Society and medical groups need to draw up appropriate guidelines for these situations, and we as patients and our relatives have the right to refuse to allow this to take place for ourselves or for our loved ones.

Donation

Kidney donation is very common and many other organs are used in transplantation. Sometimes the only way of helping a patient may be to consider using a live donor, who could survive and function normally on one kidney. If anything were to happen to that one remaining kidney, then the donor could be in serious trouble, so it is important that doctors explain very carefully the risks, as well as the benefits of live donation.

This kind of donation is only permitted by families for families. Patients need to make sure they understand that such an operation is not for their benefit and that it might have serious consequences for them later in life, if they were involved in an accident or had kidney problems. Doctors must make sure that no live donor is under undue family or emotional pressure or blackmail.

Families can and do pressurise adults to donate tissue or organs. Children and the mentally ill are even more vulnerable in such situations. Not only does such a procedure involve pain and distress to the individual, there cannot be proper consent given in such circumstances. Many would feel that we should forbid this procedure altogether. Others feel that a child may wish to help a brother or sister and should be free to do that. None of us can predict whether a child donor might grow up resenting a donation or angry that it was not allowed to happen.

Certainly, a child must be and is free to refuse to take part in such donations. Only if a child can understand what is involved, the risks and the possible consequences, and is genuinely free from family pressure should such live donations proceed. If the child's own health is put at risk by such an operation, it should not take place.

Very young children or neonates must likewise be protected. Problems do arise where it is possible to use the organs of babies who are born without proper brains (anacephalic). In a similar way to having a baby in order to provide tissue or organs for another child, the organs can be removed from anacephalic babies. Normally the same rules apply as to other donors, where families are approached and give or withhold consent. Most of us would regard having babies simply to produce organs for others or using handicapped babies in an 'organ-farming' way as wrong.

The most widely used form of organ donation uses organs which come from those who are dead. In Intensive Care or Therapy Units, many families have to consider what should happen to the organs of the dead person once irreversible brainstem death has been pronounced. Even in a desperately sad, apparently pointless situation of death, some good might come to others by organ donations. For those organs to be kept in good shape, then it may be necessary to keep the body on a machine in intensive care. It must be crystal clear that everything possible has been done for the person who has died before a doctor seeks to preserve and then remove their organs for the benefit of someone else. Ideally, we patients ourselves should express our willingness for organ donation. Carrying a card is the main way of giving consent for our organs to be used. In addition, we should discuss what we want to happen with our doctors and with our families. They can give some indication of what we would want when we are no longer able to express our wishes. Likewise, if we definitely do not want our organs to be used after our death, we should make that plain. If there are no relatives to make sure our wishes are respected and followed, then the medical profession has no right to use our bodies and organs. Different cultures, religions and traditions affect our attitudes towards organ donations. It is important that doctors are informed of our views.

Fetal Tissue

In the search for a cure for Parkinson's disease, use has been made of brain tissue from aborted fetuses. In Birmingham, some work has been done in this area and the issue of who gives consent for the use of tissue has been debated. It seems slightly odd that a woman having an abortion, particularly if she wants to get rid of the fetus, should be the one to give consent. Following the idea that parts of our body belong to us and that parents can give consent for what happens to their children, the Polkinghorne Committee[7] suggested that the use of any fetal tissue should be governed by the consent of the mother. She should only be given a 'general idea of the kinds of ways such material might be used and not given exact detail'.

There should be a clear separation between the doctors who care for the woman in her abortion and those who use the tissue, so that there is no undue pressure or role confusion on the part of the doctors. The danger is that doctors might begin to perform abortions in a way that helped preserve the fetal tissue for transplantation and research purposes, rather than in the best interests of the woman having the abortion. This is wrong and must not be allowed to happen. Some women were keen to have a baby simply to provide fetal material to help a family member who had Parkinson's. This is not permitted and hospital settings where fetal tissue is used must make sure that there is no direct link between the abortion and the use made of the tissue collected in that way.

Our Own Tissue

When we have an operation and our tissue is removed, we expect that it is simply destroyed. It might not be. It might be used in research, teaching, or even developed commercially. In a famous case in California (*Moore* v. *Regents of the University of California*, 1990) Mr Moore had his spleen removed because of leukaemia. Later, blood and bone marrow were also taken. These were used to develop a new cell line, which may make a very great financial profit. The debate in court was over who owned the tissue. The courts ruled in favour of the doctor who developed the new idea, but the disposal of parts of our bodies is still subject to our consent. For us to give consent, we need to know what uses will be made of our tissue. As patients we have the right to know what will happen to our bodies and parts of our bodies and, if we are unhappy with any uses, we are free to refuse to allow this to happen.

In some countries, like France and the United States, patients are paid for what they donate, for example, blood, placenta, sperm or eggs. This has never been the custom in the United Kingdom, where the principle of free donation as a gift for the benefit of others has been both the basis of the practice and the motive behind it. This will be an increasing area of debate and the Nuffield Bioethics

Committee are currently considering this and other similar questions. Society and doctors need clear guidelines which will preserve the principle of patient consent.

Consenting with Serious Consequences

Some surgical procedures have serious and irreversible consequences. Sex-change operations, some brain surgery, and sterilisation are usually irreversible. Giving consent in these situations needs to be carefully checked and monitored. In situations where this is happening to a child or the mentally incapacitated, doctors must consult the law courts for permission to proceed.

In the treatment of fertility, consent of the individual being treated must be given, but such treatments will have consequences for the husband, wife or partner of the person. In the past, doctors used to obtain consent from the husband or wife. This is no longer the case, but it is wise for patients to discuss such procedures which affect their fertility with their sexual partners.

When considering having children, couples may be offered genetic screening. The results of such tests may be significant for other members of the family. That information cannot be given to a family member without the explicit consent of the person tested. Doctors will encourage patients in these circumstances to allow contact to be made and will support them in that process.

In cases of dispute over paternity, genetic tests can determine who the genetic father is. It is not enough for a paternity test to be requested by a woman herself. There will be consequences for the child and for the genetic father and any other person who may be thought to be the father. This situation is usually subject to a court decision and any patient considering such a test must think of the likely impact on their relationship with the 'father' and with the child, as well as the impact on these individuals. Our giving or withholding consent can have serious implications for other people.

The Law

A patient has the right to decide what happens to his or her own body, and a doctor is open to the charge of battery or negligence if treating or examining a patient against his or her will. Doctors are advised to obtain written consent for treatments or examinations for any procedure carrying substantial risk or side effects. 'A Guide to Consent for Examination or Treatment' by the NHS Management Executive (1990) deals with this issue. A consent form is *evidence* that the nature, purpose and consequences of procedures have been explained to and understood by the patient. Doctors have a legal duty to warn of risks of treatment and to provide information on alternative options available.[8] The amount of information given is still subject to the doctor's professional discretion, but he or she must not lie regarding the information given and must respond to the questions asked by patients.

The right to refuse treatment

A patient has the right to refuse all or part of a treatment. The doctor should give a detailed explanation of the consequences of that refusal and record the patient's decision, preferably with a witness. In the case of Jehovah's Witnesses refusing treatment, the patient should be asked to sign a document saying he or she understands the increased risks incurred. The Children Act 1989 (section 5.8(1)) states that children of Jehovah's Witnesses can become wards of court if they are being medically treated against their parents' wishes.

In emergencies, doctors can give treatment to preserve the life, health or well-being of a patient who lacks the ability to give consent to treatment. The doctor is immune from liability in these situations, and it is the doctor's duty to treat in the best interests of the patient, but treatment must be limited only to what is necessary.

The Human Organ Transplants Act 1989 prohibits commercial dealings in transplantation. It also states that a person is guilty of offence if they 'remove from a living person an organ intended to be transplanted to another, or transplants an organ removed from a living person into another person who is not genetically related, unless approved by Unrelated Live Transplant Authority (ULTRA)'. The ULTRA criteria are that: no payment may be made; the referring doctor has clinical responsibility for the donor; the doctor must have explained the nature of the procedure and the risks involved, and the donor must understand both; consent must not have been coerced or obtained by an offer of inducement; the donor understands that consent may be withdrawn.

According to section 1(1) of the Human Tissue Act 1961, in the case of deceased donors, the patient must have given written or oral consent for donation in the presence of two witnesses. Section 1(2) states that the consent of relatives may also be used as criteria for donation from a deceased person if there is no reason to believe that the deceased expressed objection to donating or the surviving spouse or relatives object to the donation.

Death in hospital

If a person dies in hospital, the Area Health Authority or Board of Governors responsible for the institution are 'lawfully in possession' of the body until the next of kin ask for it.[9] The person 'lawfully in possession' of the body is under no obligation to authorise tissue removal. If removal does take place, it can only happen after a registered medical practitioner is satisfied by examination of the body that life is extinct.[10] While there is no legal definition of death, the working standard is brainstem death.

Intimate searches and prisoners

The Police and Criminal Evidence Act 1984 deals with 'intimate searches' (section 55), which are defined as 'a search which consists of physical examination of a person's body orifices' (section 118). A registered doctor or nurse can perform such a search only if an officer, at least of the rank of superintendent, has reasonable grounds for believing that the person being searched is concealing an article which would cause physical injury to another detained person or others at the police station, or that the person is concealing a Class A drug which he intends to supply or to export, and that in either case an intimate search is the only practicable means of removing it. The search must take place in hospital and be recorded.

Medical treatment is required for a prisoner if they appear physically or mentally ill, are injured, show no signs of awareness, fail to respond to conversation (unless drunk), or appear to need treatment for other reasons.

The court may order the examination of someone if notified by a medical practitioner that he is suffering from a notifiable disease, or carrying an organism that is capable of causing a notifiable disease. According to the Public Health (Control of Disease) Act

1984 this examination can be ordered in the interest of the person, his or her family, or the public. Section 37 provides compulsory removal to hospital for those with notifiable diseases after a ruling by a Justice of the Peace.

Removal orders

The National Assistance Act 1948 provides for removal orders for those persons with grave chronic diseases or those who are physically incapacitated and who are unable to look after themselves or are not being cared for properly.

The Department of Health issued guidelines for Local Research Ethics Committees (LRECs) in 1991 regarding research. Approval of LRECs must be obtained for any project involving NHS patients, fetal material and in vitro fertilisation with NHS patients, the recently dead in NHS premises, present or past access to the NHS patients' records, and access to NHS premises.

The Medical Research Council states the three basic elements for consent in regard to research are: the information given, the capacity to understand it, and the voluntariness of any decision. Patients must have information about the nature and purpose of the proposed research even if it is a basic procedure.

Embryo research

In 1991 the Human Fertilisation and Embryology Authority took responsibility for supervising embryo research, deriving its power from the Human Fertilisation and Embryology Act 1990. This Act states that consent must be given by the donor for gametes or embryos to be used in research. Any project using embryos or gametes must relate broadly to one of the following aims of research: to promote treatment of infertility, increase knowledge about the causes of congenital disease, increase knowledge about the causes of miscarriage, develop better contraception methods, develop methods for detecting gene or chromosome abnormalities in embryos before implantation, or to increase and apply knowledge about the creation and development of embryos.

In this chapter, we have examined the nature of the doctor–patient relationship and stressed that it is a partnership. The various issues which centre on the giving and refusal of consent have been explored. Respect for the patient is central to the successful doctor–patient relationship and that means proper attention to seeking and obtaining consent. It also means careful protection of confidentiality.

Questions about Consent

Choosing a Doctor

Have I explored all the available doctors in my area?

Have I read all the practice leaflets?

Why do I want to change or move doctors?

Seeing the Doctor

Have I told the doctor *all* the relevant symptoms and problems I have?

Has the doctor clearly explained what is wrong with me?

Do I understand all that the doctor has told me?

Am I clear of what different treatments are available?

Are the likely results of these treatments clear?

Which treatment if any do I want to have?

Do I want the doctor to decide for me?

Have I made that clear?

Are there any questions, worries or fears I still have?

Are there things I don't want to know?

Have I made it clear to the doctor that I don't want to know everything?

Will I do exactly what the doctor says e.g. finish the whole course of treatment?

If I live in an institution or in a prison, have I been pressurised to see the doctor?

Do I want students to be present while I am examined?

Do I mind the consultation being video-taped?

Treatment
Have I given consent for this treatment?

Has the doctor explained why I need this treatment?

Has the doctor explained what will happen?

Have I been under pressure to agree to this treatment?

Do I really want to have this treatment?

Am I happy to face the likely consequences of this treatment?

Do I want the doctor to decide what is best for me?

Have I made this clear to the doctor?

Do I want to stop this treatment?

Have I made my decision to stop clear to the doctor?

Insurance or Job Medicals
If the doctor is examining me for an insurance or employment medical, do I know what will happen to the information I give or which the doctor discovers?

Have I made it clear that I want to know everything which concerns my health?

Am I clear why the doctor is doing what he or she is doing?

If I have kept back some information, do I realise what effect that will have on the doctor's diagnosis and treatment?

If I have signed a form for the insurance or new employer to contact my GP, do I realise that everything in my record might be given?

Research
Have I been properly invited to take part in this research project?

Have the purposes and aims been explained?

What will be discovered, tested or proved by this research?

Has the doctor pressurised me to take part?

Have I given written permission?

Do I understand the form and all the information contained?

Notes to Chapter 1
1. 'Rights and Responsibilities of Doctors', *British Medical Journal* (1992), 18, 2.1.
2. *Sidaway* v. *the Board of Governors of the Bethlem Royal Hospital and the Maudsley Hospital* (1985), A.C. 871 (1985) 1 AER 643.
3. *See* P. Anderson, 'In the Genes or in the stars? Children's competence to consent', *Journal of Medical Ethics*, 18 (1992), 119–24.
4. Re T (1992) 4 A11 ER 649.
5. Re F (1990) 2 A.C. 1; *sub nom F* v. *West Berkshire Health Authority* (1989) 2 AER 545.
6. Re R (A Minor) (1991) 4 A11 ER 177; *see also* Re J (A Minor) (Medical Treatment) (1992) 4 A11 ER 614.
7. 'Review of the Guidance of the Research Use of Fetuses and Fetal Material', Cmnd 762 (London, HMSO, 1989).
8. *Sidaway, op. cit.*
9. DHSS Circular HSC (IS) 156.
10. Section 1(4) of the Human Tissue Act 1961.

2

CHOICE AND CONFIDENTIALITY

The relationship and partnership between doctors and patients depends on mutual trust and confidence. The doctor trusts the patient to tell the truth and to follow the advice given. The patient trusts that the doctor is acting in his or her best interests. One crucial element in maintaining the doctor–patient partnership is confidentiality. When we as patients tell a doctor intimate details about past, present or future, and when the doctor examines us and our bodies and discovers intimate things about us, the patient believes that the doctor will keep that information secret. This tradition of confidentiality and medical secrecy goes back to the early codes of medical ethics, which stressed that what doctors learned because of their privileged position should be kept secret. Part of the point in such confidentiality is to encourage each of us as patients to give full and frank information about ourselves to help the doctor understand all the relevant facts and factors. If we thought that what we told the doctor would be made public, we might be much less willing to reveal embarrassing details of our lives and much more careful with what we said to doctors. Confidentiality means that doctors are better able to do their job, because they are confident that patients are not keeping things back from them. As patients we need to be sure that our secrets are being kept secret. Confidentiality is so important that doctors will observe it even after our death.

This stress on confidentiality rests on the integrity of the individual. Who and what we are and our personal hurting is private. We can choose to reveal these private matters or not. Thus, self-determination and choice are at the heart of the rights of patients to control what information about us we will pass on to doctors or other professionals. Problems may arise, however, once that information is communicated to someone else. We will not be able to control what they do with that information. They may write it down or put it on a computer and other people may have access to that information. This brings us to the matter of patients' records and reports. Most of us are less concerned with what doctors might say to other people about us than with what they write down and who may read it. We live in a society where the protection of personal data is considered to be very important indeed. Doctors have to conform to these standards.

Doctors' and Patients' Attitudes to Confidentiality

There may be quite a difference between how doctors and patients regard confidentiality. When a patient tells a doctor some personal detail, then the assumption is that it is private and confidential to the doctor. If we think about it, then this is often not the case. The doctor might write it down to read. Indeed, in most general practices and hospital units, doctors talk to each other. They usually talk about patients. Sometimes this is absolutely necessary because they have to make sure that each doctor knows what is happening to a patient so that the patients can be cared for all the time. It is clearly in our best interests to have doctors share information about us with each other. It must also be said that doctors are ordinary people too and can simply gossip. Doctors do need to be more careful about what they say about us patients, especially if it is not necessary for colleagues to know certain facts. Most doctors work in settings where there are secretaries, filing clerks, administrators, nurses and other staff. Some of these people may have access to the files and records of patients. If this is the case, the doctor in charge is responsible for making sure that these people observe confidentiality. In a village, it would be very embarrassing if the local receptionist knew all the intimate details about each and every patient.

It is no surprise then that society is gravely concerned to protect the privacy of the individual and information about that individual. A first step in that direction was the decision to allow patients to see the files and notes made about them. Doctors are not allowed to write things about us in our medical notes, without allowing us the freedom and opportunity to see these notes. In any business or institution, when reports are written about us, we should have the right to see these notes and to comment on them. Certainly, annual job reviews quite commonly include an opportunity for the person being reviewed to read the report and to give assent or dissent to what has been said. In medical practices, such a freedom to have access to our medical records has raised issues of who owns the notes and who controls the information contained in them. These issues are dealt with in the Access to Health Records Act 1990 and the Access to Medical Reports Act 1988.

Not an absolute requirement

Confidentiality is, however, not an absolute requirement. Doctors are subject to the law of the land and can be required by a court to reveal information about patients. This will be examined in more detail on page 62. Such breaches of confidentiality only happen because a crime may have been committed or because it is argued that it is in the public interest to reveal what is secret. Doctors are sometimes put in very difficult situations. They may be told or discover something about a patient, for example that he is abusing a child. It is certainly in the child's and in the public interest that this information should be revealed and acted on. If the doctor does breach confidentiality, then that patient might be less willing to trust doctors again. He might feel that he cannot trust a doctor to keep a secret and so refuse to tell the doctor even things that might be very important in his future treatment and care. Other people might also be concerned that confidentiality has been broken and begin to wonder when it might happen to them. Confidentiality and confidence in the medical profession is a very fragile plant and can easily be harmed both for the individual and the community. It is ironic that revealing information by breaking confidentiality in the interest of the public good, may lead to public harm as other people may be less willing in their turn to give confidence to doctors. This is the fear in dealing with people with AIDS or who are HIV positive. If their confidentiality is breached, then those of us who might be at risk may be unwilling to be tested or even to go to consult a doctor, lest other people find out.

Limits of confidentiality

Most of us have nothing to fear from this threat to our confidentiality from public interest. In a professional situation, doctors are required to keep confidential what we tell them and they discover. Of course, many of us will meet doctors socially and then the same kind of general rules apply to what is said as in any other social setting. The bias must be towards confidentiality, but that does not mean that doctors may not reveal anything about their patients. Most of the information about us, our health and diseases, is harmless and may be shared as is appropriate. That means that we should be asked as patients to give consent and to know what uses the information will be put towards and who will have access to it. The doctor is required to justify disclosure. The fact that disclosure requires justification shows that confidentiality and privacy are the usually expected courses of action. Other doctors will need to know what is happening to us as patients if they are to have any role in caring for us and helping in treatment. When it comes to other people, like administrators and general health workers, who do not need to know any details about us, then information which identifies us and can be linked to us should be kept confidential.

Notifiable diseases come under the rubric of the law – the Public Health (Control of Disease) Act 1984 – and are examined on page 62. Doctors there are faced with competing responsibilities to the individual patient and the risk of harm to others. A doctor might be charged with negligence if he or she failed to act on confidential information which was clearly in the public interest to be known and acted upon.

These are, however, more general threats, not least because of changes within the health services and the growth and development of information technology and computer records.

Information about Us

Details about us and our health are not used just by doctors who are treating us directly. One of the roles of the doctor is to act as a medical examiner or referee for job, insurance, mortgage and loan applicants. They may also be involved in medical reports for pension schemes or state and local council benefits and housing. Without such medical reports, we as patients might not be successful in this request. Information about us is given to someone else for our benefit. It should only be done with our specific consent. We need to be clear what information will be passed on and what will happen to it once it is out of the doctor's control.

Some commercial firms, governmental organisations, academic institutions and researchers may want to know details about us as patients. Often this information is available on computer and that might mean a whole variety of people being able to read about us and discover things we would rather they did not know. Patient confidentiality must be protected, especially where the information involved is identifiable and public knowledge could be harmful to the patient. All doctors use telephones to leave messages and instructions. Radio and television are increasingly being used for teaching and sending medical information and not just in isolated communities where great distances are involved and medical availability is limited. This inevitably puts confidentiality at greater risk and considerable care must be exercised by doctors as they communicate about patients by words or pictures.

Types of Information and Records

What our doctor knows about us is not just written down. It is also in his or her head. There will be our medical records of visits to the doctor, diseases we have had, and treatment we have been given. These may be hand-written or computerised. They may include X-rays and test results, and may even include tapes and videos. In my own case, I suffer from a sleeping disorder and spent some nights in hospital being recorded. These tapes and videos are part of my medical history and are kept as a record. Such tapes, like photographs, might be useful in teaching and in research. Whatever the nature and type of information about us and the means of recording it, none of it should be made public without patient consent. If, in an extreme case of public interest, the doctor is willing or required by law to breach confidentiality, this must be explained to each patient and every effort made to persuade the patient to give consent.

When dealing with written information, computerised records, photographs or video material of patients, doctors must conform to the Data Protection Act of 1984. Maximum confidentiality is the responsibility of the doctor. Only what is necessary should be stored, and in sharing any information the 'need to know' principle should be used. Consent for the use and sharing of information must be obtained whenever feasible. If doctors want or need to take photographs or video patients, it should be done with consent, unless a crime is involved. In the case of children, professional people with recognised accreditation should be used and such photography or video-recording should not be identifiable with a particular person. When children grow up, they are free to withdraw the consent given by parents for the continued use of such material. In the same way, in mental illness when a person recovers, there is the right to have visual material about them destroyed if that is the patient's wish.

Medical textbooks, lecture notes and slides do contain pictures of patients. Ideally these pictures should not be identifiable and the patient's consent not only gained, but checked every few years. Consent is not a blanket, once-for-all event. There may come a time when a patient changes his or her mind and decides that information about him or her should be confidential. To maintain confidentiality requires vigilance and effort on the part of doctors and costs money. It is money well spent and a worthwhile effort. To safeguard the partnership between doctors and patients there must be confidence in the confidentiality of the doctor.

Whose records are they?

When doctors take notes and write down things about us, whose notes are these? (The Access to Health Records Act 1990 goes some way towards answering this question.) Some would argue that as they are facts about us as patients, they belong to us. The reality is that patients' notes are not just factual records, but also certain doctors' interpretations and reflections on those facts. In that sense, the doctor 'processes' the information received in order to make a clinical judgement and record what is necessary about the facts and the response to these facts. Doctors are quite clear that these notes belong to them. The Government and the Department of Health disagree. They argue that they belong to the Government through the agency of the Family Health Services Authority. The debate between the two views continues, with the doctors arguing that information about patients should be controlled by the patients and not by the National Health Service as a whole. While the debate runs on, we as patients should make sure that we exercise our right to see these notes and read what has been written about us.

Issues of Access

We as patients have the right to see our medical records, according to the Access to Health Records Act 1990. In the past, these records were kept secret even from the patients themselves. Such a system is open to abuse and doctors might have and did write unacceptable and inappropriate things about some of us. The atmosphere has changed now and the emphasis on the doctor–patient partnership is on being open and frank. One thing which still bothers doctors is that, in their judgement, some patients may actually be harmed by reading their notes or by finding out certain things about themselves. They may worry and be so badly distressed that they become unable to cope and function properly. It would be bad for them to know. This is a difficult area, for all of us as competent patients have the right to free access to our records. Some of us may choose not to see them, realising that it might not be good for us and that we do not want to know anyway. A good doctor should gently explain the possible risks and problems as he or she helps us make up our minds about what we want to do.

The law requires GPs to record details of illnesses which affected genetically related relatives in each other's notes. This raises a real problem over confidentiality. In order to benefit and care for one relative, details of another relative will be recorded in the other person's notes and could be read by that person. Doctors are required to protect people and that may mean breaching confidentiality. In cases where a partner refuses to reveal his or her HIV status to their spouses, the General Medical Council (GMC) warns doctors that they must break confidentiality where someone else's life is at risk. The same principle applies in relation to medical records.

We do have to recognise that doctors may be liable to prosecution and that may become clear as a result of reading medical notes. Just because a doctor may be embarrassed or in danger of legal action is not considered a good enough reason to refuse a patient access to his or her notes. All of us as patients who are competent have that right of access to our medical records.

Competent to have Access

Parents and children

Who then is competent to have access to medical records? In most cases it is obvious whether we are competent or not. The simple test used is whether a person is able to understand what it means to have access to health records. If they do understand, then they have the right of access. Parents, too, have the right of access to their children's files, except where this might conflict with the best interests of the child. If a child is able to give consent for parents to have such access, then such consent should be asked for. If refused, then parents do not have the right of access, even to their own child's notes. There is clearly in our society fundamental disagreement over whether the rights of the parents or of the child should come first. The debate seems to be leaning towards the welfare and best interests of the child, as can be seen in the Children Act 1989. If a child gives information, which he or she thinks and expects will be kept confidential, then that should be honoured. The awful reality of child abuse shows that parents do not always care for their children properly and that sometimes children have to be protected from their parents. If a child reveals a pattern of being abused by parents and the doctor records this in the notes, then the child must be protected not just by informing the authorities, but by having the information kept confidential from the parents in the event of a legal case.

As children grow up and mature they are given greater freedom and responsibility. The sexual behaviour of young people is a cause for concern in society. Doctors are often confronted with a young woman seeking advice about contraception, making it clear that she does not want her parents to know about this action. The law has decided that the rights of the young person are more important than the rights of the parents (as set out in the Children Act 1989). Doctors have to make a decision about whether the young woman is competent and sufficiently mature. Most feel that if a young person is mature enough to seek contraceptive advice, then they must pass the test of competency. Doctors must explore whether the young person really does understand what they are doing, and it may be that there is pressure from a boyfriend, peer group, or even an abusing parent. Parents do not have the right to know that the doctor has prescribed contraceptives for their child. The British Medical Association (BMA) is so committed to the principle of confidentiality for young people that they advise a doctor that confidentiality can only be broken if serious harm may result from the parents not being involved and if the young person is unlikely to be mature enough to avert such harm. If the doctor is convinced that it is in the best interests of a young person to have contraceptives prescribed and that there is enough maturity to understand the implications of what is happening, then the doctor is advised not to break confidence.

The mentally sick

In caring for mentally ill, incompetent or disordered people, the courts may appoint someone to look after their interests. That inevitably means the court may have to know confidential details about a patient. Just because a person is mentally incompetent, permanently or temporarily, does not change the rules of confidentiality. Even after we die, our notes should be kept confidential, unless there is some need to know on the part of our representatives or in the case of a legal claim. Some insurance companies write to doctors for access to confidential patient records if someone dies soon after taking out an insurance policy. There may be a fear of fraud. Doctors are obliged not to reveal such information, but this refusal might mean that the insurance company in its turn refuses to meet a claim. Insurance companies are responsible for entering into a contract. At that time they should make sure of all the relevant health details they need to make an appropriate policy decision. If there is any obvious likelihood that this kind of situation will arise, a doctor should try to discuss what the patient wants to happen. The same rule of consent should apply to any release of confidential information.

In work settings, where there may be health risks to other people, employers need to know about a patient's relevant medical problems. This should be done with the consent of the employee. A similar situation arises where the Government wishes to check up that a GP has claimed properly for treatments performed. This means access to relevant health details of patients, but should only cover the necessary information. Confidentiality should not be broken.

Some Hard Cases

In dealing with infertility, the anonymity of donors has been guaranteed. Their names are kept confidential, but there is a central register kept by the Human Fertilisation and Embryology Authority. When someone is over eighteen and wishes to marry, they are able to consult that register to make sure that their intended spouse is not genetically related to him or her. If a child is born disabled, then the donor may be traced from the register. In practice, it seems that at eighteen, people have the right to know about their genetic origins but not to know their genetic parent. The anonymity and confidentiality of donors arose out of the fear that they would not provide their sperm or eggs if they were to be traced many years later by any children produced. Recent evidence suggests that this is not the case and that people may be more willing to be known than is generally thought. It is certainly odd, and some would say unjust, that adopted children have the right to know their natural and genetic parents, while children conceived using donor sperm or eggs do not have that right, according to the Human Fertilisation and Embryology Act 1990. This is under review and may change so that anyone who donates may be asked to give consent for children to trace them. This is not the current practice, but opinion seems to be moving in this direction.

Security of Information

Doctors are directly responsible for the safety and security of information about us as patients. This responsibility covers everything from not leaving notes in the car to ensuring that files are not left open. The advent of fax machines can create problems. A lawyer approached me for advice about a legal case where a doctor was allegedly sexually involved with a number of women. I was asked if there were medical ethical issues at stake. A fax was sent outlining some intimate details of the case. It arrived in a public place, where anyone passing by could have read it. Doctors must make sure that due care and attention is given to the security of information which is telephoned, written, faxed or on computers.

The transfer and disclosure of that information comes under the law of the land and is explored below.

Special Problems for Some Doctors

If a doctor is employed by a firm, the armed forces or the prison service, then issues of confidentiality may arise. An occupational physician may have records of people who have left their jobs or died. The files still exist and it may not be possible or practical to send them on to another doctor. In such circumstances doctors are advised to retain the files for a considerable time.[1] Confidentiality should be preserved wherever possible. If it is at risk and there is no clear setting for the files to be safeguarded, then the records will be destroyed.

Prisoners and members of the armed forces both lose a certain amount of their rights to privacy and confidentiality. Those in authority need to know about the health status of those for whom they are responsible. Doctors will have to give the appropriate information to officers and governors. What is unacceptable is situations where the HIV status of prisoners might be publicly displayed on their cells. Doctors should try to ensure the maximum privacy and confidentiality of patients, even in settings where there has been a recognised limiting of individual rights.

Confidentiality and Consent

The information held by doctors about us as patients should only be what is necessary, and kept for a specific purpose which is known and agreed by us. The doctor has a responsibility to make sure that we understand not just what that information is but what significance it may have for us and what the results will be of others knowing about it. All of us as patients must give consent and authorisation for the uses made of confidential information. It is likely that there will soon be some Europe-wide safeguards of the privacy and confidentiality of information in a data protection law.

When Doctors may Disclose Confidential Information

Information about us as patients is held by a doctor for our benefit and to enable proper medical care to be given. There are, however,

circumstances when a doctor can disclose confidential information
to other people. These circumstances are: when the patient gives
permission; when it is in the best interests of the patient even if
the patient is unable to give consent; when the law requires it, as
in cases of notifiable diseases or risk to public health; when a crime
like murder has been committed; when national security is at stake;
for permitted and approved medical research.

In *job or insurance applications,* patients often ask their doctor to
release information about them to a third party. The doctor must
do that but should warn a patient if there is something in the notes
which will be disclosed and which may have bad consequences for
the patient. We may not always realise what an insurance company
or new firm will be told about us and often patients do not
even ask to see the reports written about them. Doctors should
encourage patients to read these reports.

Lawyers often ask doctors for permission to see a patient's notes
in connection with *a legal case.* Doctors should check with the
patient concerned and have consent before releasing such information. Patients need to know that the lawyers will usually ask
for the full records to be available and that these will in turn be
open to other people involved in the court case. Doctors usually
inform each other if they are about to release medical records
in which a colleague has made notes. They must certainly inform patients that this is happening.

In the past, *families and those who cared for a patient* were often
told things about the patient, without the patient knowing either
the information or that others had been told. Circumstances may
arise where a patient is not able to understand confidential information about his or her situation or may be unwilling to have that
information. This can be a problem in hostels, where a wide range
of people may care for mentally incapacitated patients and learn
that they are HIV positive. Carers must be protected, but there
may be simple measures which can be taken without having to
breach confidentiality. Only people who genuinely need to know
should be given such private details.

If a patient can understand but does not want to have information, doctors may feel that they should inform close relatives.
Patients should not be forced to know things about their illness

and what will happen, unless they wish to know. This can be particularly difficult when someone is terminally ill. Social security benefits are available for those who have less than six months to live, but require some medical report. The person involved might not know their time is so short, because they do not want that information. To establish financial and support needs, the local doctor will have to provide information about the patient's case to the authorities and this will inevitably involve those who care for the patient. The doctor must be clear that it is in the best interests of the patient to break confidentiality.

Victims of abuse, whether young or old, may not wish other people apart from their doctors to know, be involved in, or act on the knowledge of their situation. Victims may feel that if some action is taken then they might be worse off and maltreated even more severely. The doctor's primary obligation is to the person who is being abused and special attention should focus on those who are at risk or where there is any suspicion of abuse. Case conferences about such abuse do create problems for some doctors. Social workers, local authority representatives, teachers, parents, and even the child or elderly person might be in attendance. If the doctor reveals all that is confidential, there may be no way of protecting the individual or the privacy of the information about the individual. Some doctors will ask for a private session with the chair of the conference or write a private letter outlining the problems on a confidential basis. The key concern for doctors must be the well-being of the patients. The doctor should only reveal private information if there is no other way of protecting the interests of the patient. The doctor may do this even if the patient is unable or unwilling to give consent, if the situation is sufficiently serious.

In *criminal and legal cases*, doctors must answer the questions posed by a judge. The doctor should explain why confidentiality is important in the particular case, but cannot refuse to give evidence if required to do so by law. Trickier situations arise when a crime may be about to happen or harm might be done to others. Some fear that doctors might then be legally liable because of failing to inform those concerned, even if that would mean breaching confidentiality. The doctor must make a clinical decision about the best interests of his or her patients, remembering that there is a duty on doctors to protect the public from serious risk and danger. Someone with a serious history of epilepsy may not be safe to drive. If he or she refuses to inform the authorities, then a doctor may be justified in contacting the Driver and Vehicle Licensing Centre (DVLC). Doctors must be able to defend whatever decision they make, especially if it breaches confidentiality without the consent of the patient.

People with AIDS and who are HIV positive suffer from discrimination in all kinds of ways if people discover their situations. It is only to those who are genuinely at risk that a doctor has the responsibility of giving confidential information, in accordance with the GMC 'Guidelines on HIV Infection and AIDS' issued in May 1988. This should be done with the consent of the patient. If that is refused, then the doctor must be able to defend his or her decision very carefully. We as patients only need to know that a doctor is HIV positive if there is some genuine risk to us. There is no difference between the need for confidentiality for patients and doctors. Both need to have their rights and privacy respected and preserved.

Doctors should not automatically pass on information about the HIV status of patients to each other, unless it is necessary and the patient has given permission. Similarly, doctors should encourage patients who pose a threat to others if they drive, to inform the licensing authorities. Epilepsy, dementia, diabetes, poor eyesight, heart conditions, and certain medications and treatments can affect the ability to drive. Doctors should discuss the danger of driving with such patients and encourage them to act responsibly.

The Law

In strict terms, doctors have a legal duty of confidentiality to those who consult them. Although there is no statutory right to sue another person for breach of confidentiality, the legal position can be defined from a number of decided court cases.[2] Courts will enforce this duty where information is entrusted to an individual who has an obligation not to disclose that information without consent and where protecting the confidentiality of that information is in the public interest. The GMC stresses that confidential information gained in a professional capacity by a doctor remains confidential even after the death of the patient. See 'Guidance for

Doctors on Professional Confidence', GMC November 1991. The legal position is less clear.

There are a number of exceptions to the rules of confidentiality. Doctors may break it: when a patient consents to disclosure; by order of a court; when statutory duties demand it (as in notifiable diseases); when it is in the best interests of the patient; when it is in the public interest; when sharing information with other health officials to help them treat a patient; for medical teaching and research; when it is necessary for health service management. Particular concerns arise when police officers seize medical records in the investigation of a crime; when doctors employed in prisons, the armed forces or occupational medicine have conflicting duties to employers and patients; and in cases involving sexually transmitted diseases including HIV.

Doctors may be ordered by a court to reveal confidential information. If summoned to testify, the doctor should explain before taking the oath why he or she feels that the information requested should not be revealed. The exact nature of the information required should be established and only what is necessary revealed. Doctors should follow the GMC 'Guidance for Doctors on Professional Confidence' (November 1991).

Notifiable diseases

Doctors are responsible for notifying the authorities if there is reason to believe that a person has a notifiable disease.[3] These diseases include cholera, smallpox, plague, typhus. According to the GMC guidelines issued in November 1991, a doctor may disclose confidential information to a relative or third party if it is necessary and in the best interests of the patient, unless the patient bans such communication, when the doctor must respect that wish. The GMC and BMA disagree in the case of under-age contraception. The BMA favours an almost absolute confidentiality; whereas the GMC qualifies this if disclosure might be in the best interests of the young person.

A patient's right to confidentiality is always qualified. In its 1991 guidelines, the GMC stated, 'Rarely cases may arise in which disclosure in the public interest may be justified, for example a situation in which failure to disclose appropriate information would expose the patient, or someone else, to risk of death or serious harm.' Patients with epilepsy or extremely poor eyesight who continue to drive, must notify the Driver and Vehicle Licensing Centre. If they fail to do so, the doctor may provide that information.

Common exceptions

Generally, doctors are allowed to supply the police with information about a crime without the fear of breaching confidentiality, in accordance with section 5.5 of the Criminal Law Act 1967. In most cases, the choice is up to the doctor, but in cases involving road accidents the doctor must provide the police with information regarding people's identity.[4] Doctors must also report any information they have about a person committing treason or terrorism, as set out in the Prevention of Terrorism (Temporary Provisions) Act 1984.

According to the GMC's 1991 guidelines, doctors may share information about a patient with other health professionals in trying to provide optimal care. There is a distinction between disclosing information without first seeking the patient's consent and one where consent is sought and refused. In either case, the information must be given only on a 'need to know' basis and the doctor should not offer more information than is necessary for the patient's best interests.

Information for research and medical teaching should only be used if the patient's consent has been given, or, in cases where this is not practicable, when the Local Research Ethics Committee is satisfied that sufficient reasons have been given for disclosure. Researchers should confirm that their information will be kept secure and that patients will not be identifiable. Such information should be destroyed when no longer needed. The LREC will also need to be assured that the research will be conducted in line with current codes of practice and data protection legislation, and in accordance with the Department of Health's 'Guidelines on Local Research Ethics Committees', 1991.

There are only a limited number of circumstances in which the police may be granted a warrant for access to personal medical records. This will happen only if there are reasonable grounds for believing that a serious crime like murder has been committed and that there is relevant material on the premises (Police and Criminal Evidence Act 1984).

In cases of HIV infection, the doctor may be unclear whether or not there is justification for breaching confidentiality. The patient's consent should be actively sought, but if the patient refuses then the doctor may inform the health team working with the patient if they are at risk. A doctor may consider it a duty to inform a sexual partner of the HIV patient's status regardless of the patient's wishes. See the GMC 'Guidelines on HIV Infection and AIDS', May 1988.

In conclusion, the responsibility of doctors to keep information confidential covers all doctors including researchers and medical students. High standards should be taught and practised. In the partnership of doctors and patients, we patients too have a duty to be aware of the problems doctors face and to exercise a proper responsibility for other people. With good communication and mutual sympathy and understanding many of the issues about confidentiality can be resolved.

Questions about Confidentiality

Have I made it clear that I do not want what I tell the doctor to be given to anyone else?

Has the doctor explained who will be given information about me and why?

Have I seen what the doctor has written in my notes about me?

Do I want to see what has been written about me?

Am I satisfied that the doctor is ensuring that information in the practice is kept confidential?

If the doctor tells me that he will breach my confidentiality, do I understand why and have I made my attitude clear?

What arrangements has the doctor made for the secure recording of information in computers or files?

If I am asked for a video or photograph to be taken, am I happy for this to happen and with the arrangements for my confidentiality?

Do I want my family to know certain confidential things now and after I die? Have I made that clear to the doctor?

If I am a young person, has the doctor explained his or her attitude to treating me with or without my parents' consent?

If I am donating my sperm or eggs, do I know what will happen with my personal details?

Notes to Chapter 2
1. See 'Rights and Responsibilities of Doctors', *British Medical Journal* 2.1 (1992), 56.
2. *Ibid.* 36–7.
3. *Ibid.* 41ff.
4. *Hunter* v. *Mann* (1974) 2 WLR 742 (1974) 2 AER 414.

3

FERTILITY ISSUES

At least one in ten couples who want to have children are unable to do so because of infertility. That means one in ten couples are unable to have children. While some are desperately trying to become pregnant, others are equally desperately seeking to avoid having a child. Fertility and conception are topics which strike ever deeply at the heart of who and what we are. Moral, religious and cultural questions arise when we consider the beginnings of life and how as human beings we are increasingly able to manipulate human material. All of us have parents and have lived in some kind of family and social setting. Sexual being and how we control our bodies is crucial to each of us as individuals and to the well-being and functioning of society.

What it means to be infertile, have children, be a parent, have or perform an abortion, use contraception and experiment on basic human genetic material is explored in this chapter. It also bears in mind the different views and debates in society. This often finds its focus in the clash of two sets of principles. Some base their views on the respect for and sanctity of human life and material. Others stress the rights of each individual to control his or her own body. The debate is so complex and fundamental, that the Government has used various committees[1] to produce new laws and guidelines to control technological and medical advances in these areas, for example, the Human Fertilisation and Embryology Act 1990.

Childlessness

The desire to have a child and the experience of giving birth is deep in human beings. Most of us can and do procreate all too easily. Our world suffers from overpopulation and the problems that result from that. The West has increasingly seen couples control their reproduction. That still leaves many people who want to have children unable to reproduce.

When we meet people, one of the most natural topics of conversation is what family they have. For infertile people, this is a very painful question. Society expects most of us to get married. It also expects most of us who do get married to have children. For various personal reasons, like concern about overpopulation, or career and lifestyle desires, many couples choose to remain childless. They may experience pressure from society, but by and large are happy with their decision. They can reverse it at any time, for they are fertile. It is not so easy for the infertile.

Infertility is not even regarded as an illness by many folk, for we are able to live normal, healthy lives without having children. Others would argue that having children is a normal part of human relationships between men and women, especially in marriage. Traditionally, one of the purposes of marriage was the having and nurturing of children. Family life is still at the centre of how we live as a society. Infertility may not be a disease, but it is felt and experienced as a hardship by those who are infertile. They feel disabled and their infertility can become both a physical and psychological problem. Modern medical science and technology have produced some solutions.

Male Infertility

At least one third of infertility in couples is because of problems with the male. These problems are either with the delivery system or quality control of the sperm. If the man is unable to deliver the sperm in the right place at the right time, then the solution is artificial insemination. That involves collecting sperm by masturbating. Some would regard this as an immoral act. Most people have little unease about masturbating and in a situation where the point of such an act is clearly to procreate, then some Catholic theologians argue that it is morally justified. A doctor or nurse can then deliver the sperm using a syringe. Artificial insemination by the husband (AIH) raises few moral uneases, except that it is unnatural.

There are some in society who feel that interfering with reproduction and using artificial means to create a pregnancy is wrong because it is unnatural. The problem is that almost all medicine is unnatural in the sense that it tries to put right things which have gone wrong naturally. Many doctors argue that, in fact, medicine is only trying to help nature do its job properly, efficiently and more quickly. For those who feel that assisting reproduction by using artificial means is wrong that will be the end of the matter except to help the infertile live with their infertility. Many will feel that helping nature do its job by aiding couples to have children is a proper moral and medical aim and practice. It still means drawing lines and limits.

If a man has a low or nil sperm count, then it is unlikely that he will be able to reproduce. It is possible to try to improve the sperm count by drugs and hormonal treatment. This can sometimes make a difference. An alternative is to use various techniques of collecting sperm over a period of time, and giving a massive injection may be tried, but some men simply cannot 'father' a child. Technology offers an alternative. It involves artificial insemination by donor (AID). In the United Kingdom, donors are often medical students. They are volunteers who are usually paid generous expenses instead of a fee. Their motive is often compassion for the infertile. It also could be a desire to have many children of their own or to make money. To prevent this, donors are screened and counselled about what it means to donate sperm. The number of children produced by a donor is also restricted.

Many couples are uneasy about the intrusion of a third party into their relationship. It is not adultery in the classic sense, for no sexual act or contact takes place between the donor and the woman. That does not alter the intrusion of someone else's genetic material into the situation and the fear that any child produced might be rejected by the male in the couple on the grounds that it is not 'his' child. AID is widely used and accepted. Most infertile men are happy for this kind of insemination to take place if it is the only way of having a baby.

Donors are carefully screened to avoid medical and genetic diseases. This is particularly important in an age of HIV and AIDS.

Donors are anonymous. This is to protect their privacy and to encourage people to donate. The prospect of a child arriving on your doorstep eighteen years after your donation, was felt likely to discourage donors. Anonymity means that the donor has no rights or responsibilities for what has been donated. Any children produced have no rights or responsibilities in relation to the donor. The moral implications of this for the donor and child are discussed on pages 74 to 75. A central register of donors is kept by the Human Fertilisation and Embryology Authority in the event of a child being born handicapped or having a genetic disease. Currently, that register will only be used to provide information about genetic backgrounds and not the names and identities of fathers.

In California, the setting up of a sperm bank of Nobel Prize winners raised the issue of eugenics. The nightmare scenario portrayed in Aldous Huxley's *Brave New World*, where reproduction was controlled and graded, seemed to be coming true. Couples in the UK, however, are given donor sperm which matches the characteristics of the male in the partnership as closely as possible. There is no danger that sperm from someone of a different race will be used. Because of the screening, the child produced is less likely to have a genetic disease.

Female Infertility

The problems of infertility in women are more complex. It may be the quality of the eggs or the delivery system. Surgery may be able to unblock or bypass the fallopian tubes. Hormonal treatment may help the quality of the eggs. In vitro fertilisation (IVF) means that the actual fertilisation of the egg can take place outside of the woman in a glass or petri dish. To maximise the likelihood of pregnancy, women are given drugs to make them 'super-ovulate'. They then produce a large number of eggs, for example twenty at a time. These can be removed and placed in a dish for fertilisation. Most women do not want to have twenty children at one time. Indeed, twins are very common as a result of this hormonal treatment, so that, too, points in the direction of selection. Doctors and patients are then faced with some important moral considerations.

Usually many eggs are fertilised and the best three chosen for implantation in the woman. That leaves 'spare' embryos or pre-embryos. Some people are trying to call this stage of human life pre-embryonic rather than an embryo, because without implantation there cannot be full development. Some couples feel that they should only use one fertilised egg at a time and so avoid creating extra embryos which might then be destroyed or used in experiments. Unfortunately, this seriously reduces the chances of pregnancy. Currently, it seems that the best chance of becoming pregnant is if three embryos are implanted in the womb. There is always a risk of multiple pregnancies and twinning. There might therefore be six babies developing in the womb. This can lead to embryo reduction (see page 76). What happens to the 'spare' embryos is discussed later in this chapter. One possible use is to donate them to childless couples who are unable to produce their own embryos. In such a situation, neither of the genetic parents is directly involved in the bringing up of the child by its 'social' parents. Some have likened this to an early form of adoption. Such measures raise difficult moral and legal questions about what is a parent and may create all kinds of emotional and psychological tensions in and between a couple.

If a woman is unable to develop her own eggs, then a donor might be used. Usually the donor is another woman who is undergoing fertility treatment herself and has produced extra eggs. Again that donor is carefully screened for genetic abnormalities. Only eggs which are thought to be healthy are used in egg donation. The woman receiving the egg donation may not be able to carry a pregnancy for the full nine months in spite of medical care and supervision. This then raises the possibility of using a surrogate mother or 'renting a womb'.

Surrogate Mothers

Surrogacy is a controversial and emotional issue. Concerns over the risks of exploiting women and 'buying' children have led to a banning of commercial surrogacy arrangements, as laid down in law by the Surrogacy Act 1985. It would be impossible to ban informal or family surrogacy arrangements. Doctors are advised that this should be very much a last resort and that they should be cautious about becoming directly involved. Many doctors feel that it is better that a doctor is involved to protect all those in the situation and this is recommended by the British Medical Association Working Party Report, 1990 (chaired by Sir Malcolm McNaughton). The doctor may help in the process of fertilising the surrogate mother by syringe. Once a pregnancy has been achieved, the doctor has the normal responsibility to the mother and the child. The doctor must protect the interests of the child, in particular if the doctor was actively involved in the fertilisation process. The doctor should seek to ensure that everybody involved in the situation understands the risks and dangers. Some doctors will refuse to have anything to do with such arrangements on conscientious grounds. If a doctor is willing to help, then the specific problems need to be carefully and clearly explained and handled.

Couples and the other woman involved need to think very carefully before beginning a surrogacy arrangement. All kinds of things could happen. If the surrogate mother changes her mind, she may want to keep the child. If the child is born handicapped then both the mother and the prospective parents may not want to have it. The surrogate might smoke, drink heavily and be carrying a genetic disease, all of which might seriously affect the child. The psychological and emotional trauma for the surrogate, her family and her actual and prospective partners, and, not least, to the child who is produced by these means cannot be finally known. Doctors need to make sure that a couple seeking surrogacy help are not avoiding pregnancy for frivolous means or mere personal convenience. Medical responsibility covers all those involved in and affected by the surrogacy arrangements. It should only be a last resort and will almost inevitably raise moral and practical problems both in the short and long term.

Who can be treated?

None of us has a right to have children. There is a freedom to procreate, but if we are infertile, doctors and society have no responsibility to provide us with children. There are, however, fertility treatments available and this raises questions about how many fertility centres there are and should be and who should be able to use them. In a world of too many people and at a time of pressure on limited health resources, fertility treatment is not widely regarded as very important. Rather than talking about 'needing' a child, it might be more appropriate to talk of 'wanting' children. Every clinic has some kind of criteria for who is to get fertility treatment. Obviously, this means discrimination. Not everyone who wants to have a child will or can be helped. That is not just because their particular problems with infertility cannot be solved, but that resources are limited so hard choices must be made. Most of our fertility is not controlled by others. If doctors are involved in helping people become fertile they will not just control what treatment is given but also who receives the treatment. There is no point in trying to treat those who are unable to be helped or unwilling to go through the difficult processes involved. Before a woman is given infertility treatment, the male must have his sperm tested to make sure the couple knows where the problem lies.

There is no nationally agreed set of rules for who is to be treated in infertility clinics. The Human Fertilisation and Embryology Authority (HFEA) has refused to make such criteria. The general rules are that only those who are in a stable heterosexual relationship or married will be treated. Most single women, lesbians and those who have what is regarded as an 'unsuitable' lifestyle are refused treatment.[2] The bias is in favour of traditional relationships for two kinds of reasons. Doctors are concerned that a child created to live in a homosexual or single-sex home setting may be disadvantaged, if not because of the lack of a significant male or female figure, then by the attitudes of other children and society to him or her. The other reason is that much of the funding for fertility work is by public donation. Doctors fear that support would be affected if it were known that lesbians were regularly being fertilised and treated. Doctors are faced with a hard decision. This judgement should rest on medical grounds. If a woman is not infertile, but chooses not to have normal sexual relationships with a man, it is hard to see that doctors have any moral or medical responsibility for treating her. With no disease, handicap or fertility problem, the doctor has no medical obligation to provide a service which is designed for those who are infertile.

Society does not and cannot control who becomes a patient. Nevertheless, doctors are responsible for situations in which they play a part in creating by their fertility work. While it is not impossible for those who are not married or not living in what are considered 'normal' relationships to find treatment, it is usually only the married and those in heterosexually stable relationships who are treated. Different clinics will and do have different rules. Any couple presenting for help at an infertility clinic has the right to know what these rules are. Normally, the clinic will have some written expression of its practice. Patients should read and discuss this with the clinic and their own GP. In law, clinics are controlled by the HFEA in terms of what they are permitted to do and in all their research. If a clinic breaches the rules, its licence may be withdrawn and it will not be permitted to carry on.

Who gives consent?

The basic standard for all medical treatment in the doctor–patient partnership is that the patient gives fully informed, valid consent. To be fully informed means that infertile couples need to know a great deal about the medical procedures involved in infertility. They need to understand the risks involved as well as the likelihood of success. Different clinics have very different success rates, not least because they use different techniques. Couples need to know what these techniques are and what the success rate is. These figures must be published as it is legally required by the HFEA. Patients must not be subjected to invasive or distressing treatment when there is little realistic chance of success. Doctors must ensure that patients have all the information they need, understand its significance in terms of risk and personal benefit, and then are able to make their own decision, aware that it is not just a medical matter, but has moral and religious dimensions.

The Moral Dimensions

Many regard fertility treatment as unnatural. They are uneasy about the removal of sexual intercourse from the bedroom to an artificial process in a laboratory. They argue that simply because medical technology means we are able to do certain things, like treat infertility, it does not mean that we ought to do that. Just because we can, does not mean we should. A whole host of moral and social issues are created in fertility treatments. They raise the questions of who and what is a parent. Traditionally, a parent was the biological father or mother. Medicine can separate biological from social parenting. In adoption, society has been forced to make that separation because the biological parents were unable to fulfil their responsibilities as parents. Adoptive parents become social parents and are responsible for the care and nurture of the adopted child. Fertility work creates the distinction if donors are involved.

Recent moves in the law have tended to suggest that the social father is the father of the child in order to protect the anonymity of the donor. In the case of motherhood, the woman who gives birth is regarded as the mother of the child. This makes commercial surrogacy arrangements pointless. Many are concerned that these new definitions of parenthood change our basic views of children and parent relationships. Some are also uneasy about what they regard as the failure to take seriously the motives, rights and responsibilities of donors. Donating genetic, life-giving material is viewed differently from giving blood. This seems to be more significant for women than men. Giving sperm often seems to have little significance for men. Donating an egg or carrying someone else's child for nine months is a very different and often deeply emotional experience. Currently, donors have no rights in relation to any children produced using their genetic material. Even if they later become infertile or have a partner who is infertile, they will not be able to discover who is their child.

Doctors are responsible for the patients they are treating. In dealing with infertile couples, there are three parties to be considered. Any children who result from such treatment will create a specific responsibility for the doctor. Without that medical input that child would not exist. Doctors must ensure that such children are not disadvantaged by the way they were conceived and born and the setting they will be inhabiting. Most doctors regard the interests of such children as more important than the wants and needs of the couple who seek to have a child. A couple needs to understand and to be counselled about what it means to have fertility treatment and all its implications. It would be possible for a desperate couple who had a seriously ill child to ask a doctor to help them become pregnant to create a child who might be able to donate life-saving material for the dying child.[3] Doctors in the UK would regard any such medical involvement as wrong. Children should be created for their own sakes and not simply to be used for the benefit of others.

AID and IVF children

Adopted children have the right to discover their natural parents, when they reach the age of eighteen. AID and IVF children are not so fortunate. They may not even know about their origins. Families are not good at keeping secrets. To discover accidentally that your parents are not really your parents can be devastating. The medical records of the child need to have his or her origins recorded. In the event of certain genetic diseases developing in later life, it is vital to know about and be able to trace that genetic information. Currently, the HFEA keeps a register of donors and may divulge that information if it is absolutely necessary in a legal case or where a genetic problem has arisen. At eighteen, a young person born from IVF or AID is able to discover the details of their genetic background and history, but not who is the parent. The pressure, especially in light of the Children Act 1989, seems to be moving in the direction of a child having more, rather than less, information and it seems that this may not affect the likelihood of donors being willing to continue to donate.[4]

Personal attitudes

The feelings and attitudes of the fertile partner in the treatment of the infertile person need to be noted. For the sake of any child produced and the well-being of the existing relationship, doctors must try to involve the partners in the processes of treatment. This is not only more likely to ensure greater success, it may avoid some serious breakdowns and disagreements. The use of material from a third party may have profound effects on the couple and their attitudes toward each other and the children who may be born as a result of the use of that material. If both partners understand the implications of such treatments, then they should be made aware of all the responsibilities they will have.

Fertility treatment in creating a large number of embryos creates new kinds of problems over what we should or should not do with them. If a woman has a multiple pregnancy, then that creates a greater chance of premature birth and a poor rate of survival for the children. To prevent this, doctors engage in what they call selective reduction. If six healthy embryos result from fertility treatment, then they may discuss with the couple the possibility of reducing that number to two in order to maximise the chances of ending up with two healthy babies. It seems ironic that having struggled to produce babies, doctors then destroy embryos to try to ensure that some babies will survive. Many see this as a call for finding new techniques which do not lead to multiple pregnancies and the need for selective reduction. Currently, doctors are allowed to do this with the patient's full consent. It is not without medical risk both to the mother and to the remaining embryos. There is the view that local ethics committees should be consulted and offer guidelines for this practice.

Research on Embryos

If the embryos produced are not used by the couple or donated to other infertile folk, then they may be used for research. The Warnock Report and the HFEA have discussed this and recommend various rules for such research. Much of the original and continuing debate hinges on the status of the embryo. We shall discuss this more fully in the section on abortion later in this chapter. The issue is whether or not an embryo has the rights of human beings or whether it is merely a lump of material. Most of society does not seem to believe that embryos are fully human. They are more potential persons than persons with potential. The human potential and origin cannot be denied, but how embryos should be treated is hotly debated. The reality is that embryos are being used legally for research purposes.

Warnock concluded that it was legitimate to experiment on and with embryos under certain conditions. These set limits to research up to fourteen days of development, denote conditions for the storage and development of embryos, and forbid or limit certain kinds of experimentation, like using other animals or species to act as wombs or in testing the mobility of sperm. The choice of the fourteen-day limit relates to the development of the brainstem tissue, the timing of the development of the individual rather than being a twin, and the capacity to feel pain. In the end, the benefits to the rest of us were held to outweigh the harm done to the embryos. The causes of and treatments for infertility, the testing of drugs, especially for contraception, and genetic developments have all gained from such research experiments.

There is an important difference between research on an embryo for its own benefit and research which is for the benefit of others. In the first case, we are trying to put right something that has gone wrong in the same way as we treat any other illness or disease. In the second case, we are using the embryo as a means to some other end rather than as an end in itself. To help discover how to prevent and cure genetic diseases and overcome infertility is regarded as a justification for continuing embryo research. How the issues of sanctity of life and the status of the embryo relate to the abortion debate are outlined on pages 85 to 87. The job of the HFEA is to oversee research on embryos. For such work to be permitted it has to relate to infertility, congenital diseases, miscarriage, contraception, genetic and chromosomal disorders or the development of embryos.

Genetic Research and Therapies

Perhaps the fastest growing area of medical science is genetics. There is in process an international project to map the whole genetic structure of human beings. Increasingly, we are discovering the way genetic factors are crucial in our susceptibility to and the development of disease. Already, we are able to manipulate some genetic structures, both in plant and animal work, but also in human beings. We all benefit from more and better food, but are uneasy when medical scientists begin to tamper with the very stuff of human beings. There have been major contributions to the debate over genetic research and therapy.[5]

Most doctors and scientists are convinced that genetic research and therapy should be limited to work which deals directly with tissue connected with a body. It is called somatic-cell gene therapy, which is for the benefit of the individual concerned. The same moral questions arise as in all major treatments like transplants. In contrast, there is little enthusiasm for germ-line gene therapy, which would affect not just the individual and his or her genetic make-up, but also that of his or her descendants. There are risks of genetic harm, of the loss of some as yet unknown benefits linked with a particular gene, and no way we can predict or control what happens to the gene pool. An example might help. Sickle-cell anaemia is a major debilitating disease. But the sickle-cell does seem to provide the advantage of protection against malaria. If we were to get rid of that cell line, we might remove the basis of discovering a natural immunity for a widespread disease. It is already possible to screen for an increasing number of genetic disorders using chorionic villus sampling and amniocentesis testing. To go beyond this is presently illegal.

Genetic testing and screening already happen for diseases like Huntington's chorea, cystic fibrosis and sickle-cell anaemia. This can affect both fetuses in the womb and individuals and couples considering having children who may pass on genetically related diseases. The screening process must always take place with the consent of those involved. They will also require counselling help to make sure they are able to understand and cope with the results of such testing. Such results must be confidential to the patient. This can only be set aside if there is a serious risk to the life or health of family members.

In the case of the genetic screening of features, other moral issues are raised. One couple was being tested for Huntington's chorea to see if the child in the womb was a carrier of the disease. They were given the good news that the child was perfectly normal. They then asked whether the child was a boy or a girl. The counsellor asked why they wanted to know. They said that if it was a girl they would seek an abortion. They did not want a girl. If the result had been that the child would be born abnormal, then the couple would have been offered a termination of pregnancy. This raises the moral issues of abortion and the attitude individuals and society have to handicaps and handicapped people. It is important here that by handicaps we mean some serious disease or disability. Being the 'wrong' sex is not a handicap. Frivolous reasons need to be ruled out before an abortion is suggested, far less performed. For those who are opposed to abortion on principle, there may be some help available either through the technologies of infertility treatments or from increasing medical ability to 'adjust' genetic disorders by genetic manipulation. What the science of genetics is able to do will continue to develop. Society and doctors in particular need to set clear moral guidelines and be aware of the likely moral and social consequences of such work.

Sex Selection

New techniques are developing which will enable parents to choose the sex of a potential child through assisted conception. The Human Fertilisation and Embryology Authority ask about all such new developments, 'Is this necessary or desirable?' There are two main reasons for wanting to choose the sex of a child. On medical grounds, we know that many 'sex-linked' diseases affect children. These are usually the result of a genetic problem in the mother, who passes this on to the child. Colour blindness, haemophilia and muscular dystrophy are carried and passed on in this way. If there is a history of serious inherited diseases parents may wish to have a child free of the disease. On social grounds, a couple may want to have a girl or a boy for a wide variety of reasons ranging from the desire to balance a family by having a child of the opposite sex to attaching a higher status to one sex over and against the other.

The BMA Medical Ethics Committee has been concerned about the commercial advertising and provision of such treatment where the scientific evidence is not proven and for which there is no medical justification. All of us need to consider the moral issues very carefully before using such services. Freedom of choice, the balance of the sexes in society, religious and cultural attitudes toward the sexes, and the benefit and danger of having 'designer children' will be at the heart of the debate. The more science develops, the more issues we as a society have to face and the more decisions we have to make which will affect parents, children and the national and world communities.[6]

Ante-Natal Care

Already we are in the realm of ante-natal care. Women are entitled to have access to the best pre-natal care possible. Patients have a responsibility to consult their doctors and to attend the ante-natal clinics to safeguard their own health and that of their baby. If problems arise during the pregnancy, then a scan, biopsy or even

amniocentesis may be appropriate. There are some risks involved
in biopsies and amniocentesis. The woman needs to be fully aware
of these risks before making a decision. The benefit from knowing
the state of the fetus usually outweighs the risks to the fetus and
to the woman. This is a matter of the clinical judgement of the
doctor. Doctors will not suggest such testing unless they regard it
as necessary and having a clear benefit for mother and child.

The issue of where to have the baby raises important matters of
patient choice. There is a good deal of enthusiasm for home deliveries,
'natural' childbirth and other methods of giving birth. Doctors are
often sceptical of some of these approaches and all too well aware of
the dangers of home confinement if something goes wrong. Close
liaison with midwives and health visitors is vital. Doctors should
make clear the nature and extent of their unhappiness and why
they are so concerned. In the end, the patient must make up her
own mind. A doctor may feel that he or she cannot be responsible
for a home confinement. Then the doctor is still required to attend
in an emergency situation and is still responsible for the general,
continuing health care of the woman and the family. A doctor cannot
be forced to agree to take part in a situation where the danger is
overwhelming to mother and baby. A doctor has the right to refuse
to be involved in a home confinement, but should then make sure
the midwife takes responsibility, if she is willing.

Giving Birth

The shift in the attitude to giving birth in the last few years is
dramatic. Fathers used to be kept in waiting rooms and then
confronted with the news of a safe delivery or of complications.
Now fathers are encouraged to attend ante-natal classes, to be fully
involved in helping prepare for the confinement, and to be present
at the birth. I vividly remember holding one of my wife's legs and
urging her to push, at 1.00 a.m. in a busy maternity unit, while
the midwife held the other leg and delivered the baby.

The father present at birth

If serious problems do arise, then fathers will be asked to leave,
to allow the medical and nursing staff to act quickly and without

distraction. All too many men have fainted when they realise the pain of childbirth and experience its reality. Support for the woman giving birth is vital and the father can play a key role in giving that support. Women need to know that different doctors do have different attitudes to what should happen in childbirth. Caesarean operations, the use of forceps and the cutting of the vaginal wall to ease birth (episiotomy) may be normal procedures or used only in emergencies. If a patient has strong views about the birth process, she should discuss them with the doctor. The doctor must make clear what the normal procedure and accepted practices are and make sure the woman understands the information, its implications, and gives proper consent for the doctor to do whatever is necessary. The wonder of new life never seems to be lost on medical and nursing staff and their encouragement and care of the mother and child helps greatly. Part of this may be helping with problems over breast-feeding or advice about resuming sexual intercourse. Good communication and sympathetic understanding on the part of doctors make all the difference in the experience of childbirth.

Contraception

While many people are happy to have children and some are desperately trying to become pregnant, others are doing all they can to prevent a pregnancy. Government statistics suggest that about half the conceptions in England are unwanted or unintended.[7] The UK has one of the highest number of teenage pregnancies and abortions in Europe according to the 1992 'Annual Report of the Chief Medical Officer'. A worrying number of abortions are performed on girls under sixteen.[8] This seems to point to an increasing need for sex education, information and family planning. The development of the so-called 'morning-after' Pill and post-coital drugs has blurred the distinction between contraception and abortion. This will be discussed in the section on abortion on page 85.

Some doctors and members of the public have fundamental moral objections to contraception. Some doctors do not wish to be involved in providing either contraceptive information or services. Doctors are free to refuse to take any personal part in such services, but are advised by the BMA to refer a patient who wants contraception advice to the Family Planning Association or to another doctor. This should be done as quickly as possible. The doctor has the right to express the reasons for his or her view, but should not put pressure on the patients to conform to that view.

Dealing with the Under-Sixteens

Parents are deeply concerned that their children may be using contraception prescribed by doctors without parental knowledge or consent. Since the Gillick case,[9] the standard has been set that a young person can be given such contraception if he or she is sufficiently mature and competent to understand the significance of sexual behaviour, its consequences and what is involved in contraception. Doctors are increasingly concerned about the risks of cervical cancer from sexual intercourse at an early stage in life and from multiple partners. Venereal disease, HIV and AIDS, possible pregnancies, and the long-term effects of sexual activity and the use of contraceptives should be clearly discussed with the young person. If they decide to continue, the doctor may feel that it is in the best interests of the young person to prescribe a contraceptive and prevent a pregnancy or abortion.

One key element in this is confidentiality (see the Chapter on Confidentiality and the Children Act 1989). The right of the patient to confidentiality covers both situations where the young person refuses to allow his or her parents to be informed and situations where the confidentiality of medical records needs to be protected. The doctor should make every reasonable effort to persuade the young person to communicate their situation to their parents and involve them in the decision. If the young person refuses, the doctor must focus concern on what is best for the young person who is the patient. Medical records should not be open to parents if the young person does not wish them to know about the request for contraception. Even when the doctor might refuse to give contraception on the grounds that the patient is not sufficiently mature to understand all that is involved in sexual activity and contraception, the confidentiality of the notes should be protected on the grounds that the young person expected the doctor to keep that information confidential. This puts doctors in an invidious position between parents and children. Their primary duty is to the patient who asks for their help. It is only in the extreme cases of abuse, incest or other kinds of sexual exploitation, that confidentiality can be broken by doctors, according to the General Medical Council advice issued in November 1991 – 'Guidance for Doctors on Professional Confidence'.[10]

Patients in Mental Hospitals

There has been widespread concern about the apparent indiscriminate use of contraceptives on some people in mental institutions. Those who are mentally disordered are extremely vulnerable to exploitation and abuse by other patients as well as staff. There is often a high level of sexual activity in such institutions. This is partly due to the inability of staff to supervise everyone all the time, and may even be encouraged by some staff who regard sexual activity as a normal and constructive part of a patient's life. To protect vulnerable patients, contraception may be given to those at risk. Doctors must seek consent from the patient if this is at all possible. Otherwise the issue of what is in the best interests of the patient becomes the deciding factor. This involves a clinical judgement by the doctor of the likely consequences of sexual activity without contraception and the dangers from any contraceptive measures themselves. This might include a discussion about the need for sterilisation.

Sterilisation

In normal circumstances, there are two main reasons for sterilisation. The first is to remove the ability to reproduce once and for all. The other is where some other treatment leads to or requires sterilisation. In the latter case, it is for the benefit of the patient. Before such a sterilisation takes place, the patient should be fully informed as to the necessity for and consequences of such a move. It requires fully informed consent. Sterilisation as a means of contraception is unacceptable to many, including Roman Catholics. It is a dramatic and largely irreversible process, so the doctor must ensure that a patient understands the significance of such a decision. In an age when many people remarry, they may find that they do want to have children in the new relationship. Careful thought should precede a sterilisation procedure. In the past, this could not be performed without the consent of the spouse. These days have gone, but it is good medical practice to encourage a patient to discuss sterilisation with their respective spouse or partner. It may avoid later misunderstanding and breakdown in the relationship.

In the case of those in mental institutions or with learning disabilities, sterilisation measures cause great debate. If, as seems likely in the past, some young women were sterilised without their consent and knowledge, then they were not only deprived of the possibilities of having a child, but of the possibilities of recovering from the mental illness and then being able to have children. Such sterilisations have been the subject of much legal debate, which focused on the need for and possibility of giving consent and the morality of performing an irreversible operation for no obvious direct benefit other than to prevent pregnancy. This could have been achieved without such drastic measures. To justify sterilisation, it must be clear that it is in the best interests of the patient.[11]

There does not seem to be any basic right to reproduction, as no one could have the responsibility or duty to make sure it happened. We are, however, free to reproduce. Reproductive choices seem to relate to rational choices. The ability of those whose mental capacities are limited to make such rational decisions is matched by concern about their ability to care for and bring up a child. Such judgements are too hard and important to be left to doctors alone. Doctors must seek court approval for sterilisation, unless there are clear clinical reasons for such a drastic step. This inevitably leads back to some definition of what constitutes the best interests of a person. Usually it is what is necessary to save life or what will lead to improvement in physical and mental well-being. That standard is to be assessed by what a responsible body of relevant medical opinion judges to be appropriate. For the individual doctor, as in the case of treating sex offenders, another doctor should be consulted to validate the treatment decision.

Abortion

Since 1967, when the Abortion Bill was first introduced to Parliament by David Steel MP, there has been a major shift. Public opinion was concerned to put an end to the horrors of back-street abortions and the deaths of desperate women. Now abortion is largely seen as available on demand. It has become a key plank in the women's movement and is part of the alleged right to do whatever we want with our own bodies. This begs the question at the heart of the debate about the status of the fetus and any rights of protection which should be safeguarded for the fetus by the rest of society. The over-simplified discussion seems to reduce the choice between the sanctity of life and being 'pro-choice'.

The Abortion Law
Abortions are legal in the United Kingdom if certain conditions are fulfilled. The Abortion Act carries a conscientious objection clause by which the doctor can refuse to participate in terminations but is obliged to provide necessary treatment in an emergency when the woman's life may be jeopardised. It would seem that GPs cannot claim exemption from giving advice or performing the preparatory steps to arrange an abortion.

Forms of Abortion
Surgical termination of pregnancy, either by suction or by removal, or the inducing of the labour process has increasingly been replaced by the use of drugs like RU486. These drugs can be used up to seventy-two hours after intercourse or in combinations with other drugs up to nine weeks. Some are afraid that this makes abortion too easy and has become nothing more than a later form of contraception. The failure of individuals and society to manage their sexual desires and behaviour, and a widespread view that sexual intercourse is part of human life more as recreation than for procreation, seems to have led to increasing demands for abortions if contraception fails or is not used.

Arguments in Abortion
Those in favour of abortion point to the serious harm done to women if they are forced to continue a pregnancy against their will. Few would refuse an abortion if the life of the mother was at risk. Part of living properly is to be able to make choices. Thus, abortion can be seen as an issue of a woman's control over her own body

and emphasises a right to do whatever she wishes with her own body. Doctors are not just allowed to perform abortions by law. On this view, they are morally required to act as the woman wants. If the doctor rejects such a rights-based decision, then it is argued that compassion for a woman's psychological, social and physical well-being should lead to abortion on demand.

In contrast, those opposed to abortion rest their case on the sanctity of life and the moral status of the fetus. Generally, they argue that human life begins from fertilisation, or at the very least implantation. Thus from that moment human life is present and should be preserved. Doctors are meant to be in the business of preserving life. Abortion is killing or, some claim, murder. If the law allows or tries to justify such taking of life, the law should be changed and doctors are not required to act against their consciences.

When does life begin?

There is a wide range of opinion which tries to discover some magic moment when human life begins. Fertilisation, implantation, quickening, viability, birth and even independent life have been among the contenders. The problem is that even if society did agree about when life began, it might still disagree about what duties that imposed on doctors, what rights that life should have, and how to deal with conflicting claims and other people's rights. The BMA regards the viability of the fetus as the crucial moment when a fetus becomes a fetus and therefore the doctor is required to preserve the life of both patients – the mother and child. Viability is a sliding scale, which depends on the ability of medical science to preserve life. But such a standard does provide a rule of thumb for doctors in their judgements about abortions. They are also required to obey the law.

Legal Issues

Doctors are required to advise a patient under what grounds she may have an abortion. If the doctor has moral or religious objections to abortion, there remains a responsibility to refer the patient to another doctor as quickly as possible. Patients should be aware of the views of their own doctor and check that any referral is to a doctor who will be willing to provide an abortion if it meets the legal requirements. Doctors cannot be forced to sign a consent form for abortion, though it seems that they are morally and legally bound to make a referral to another doctor.[12] It is considered professionally wrong to delay such a referral with the aim of making an abortion impossible or illegal. The rights of the patient must be preserved, even when a doctor disagrees with the course of action. If they fail to do this, they may become legally liable for their referral. In hospitals, doctors may refuse to perform abortions, but they are likely still to be expected to look after the patients before and after the operation.

The main legal control over fertility work is the Human Fertilisation and Embryology Authority. It controls and licenses centres which offer treatment using donated sperm and eggs and research on human embryos. It keeps a register of children born from such treatment and the donors involved. A child produced by these means has no access to any information which may identify a gamete or embryo donor. Under the Human Fertilisation and Embryology Act 1990, a woman who carries a child is deemed to be the mother. The woman's partner or husband is normally regarded as the child's father. While surrogacy itself is not illegal, commercial surrogacy is, in accordance with the Surrogacy Arrangements Act 1985.

Under the Offences Against the Person Act of 1861, it is a criminal offence for anyone except a registered doctor to perform an abortion. Abortions are only legal under the law if: two doctors agree; the pregnancy has not exceeded twenty-four weeks; to continue would involve great risk of injury to the physical or mental health of the woman or her existing children; if the child, when born, would suffer from serious handicap. The Abortion Act 1967, as amended by section 37 of the Human Fertilisation and Embryology Act 1990, states these conditions and the current situation as far as the law is concerned.

In conclusion, it should be realised that fertility and its control are not just matters for us as individuals or couples, but for society as a whole. The beginnings of life, like its ending, involve fundamental moral issues, attitudes and beliefs. The partnership between doctors and patients must work not just for the best interests of the patient, but for all those involved in issues of fertility, genetics and abortion. The well-being of future generations is in our hands, here and now, and we must take our responsibility for the future very seriously. Such responsibility begins at the start of life, but also is involved as babies become children and young people.

Questions about Fertility
Infertility

If we want a child and have been trying for a long time should we consult the doctor?

Do I understand what is involved in infertility treatment?

Do I understand AIH, AID and IVF?

What is my moral attitude to the fertility treatment I am being offered?

What will my and my partner's attitude be to any children born if they are biologically related to only one of us?

Do I understand what will happen to my donation or any embryos resulting from that?

Do I understand the rules of the fertility clinic about who should be treated and what research is allowed to take place?

Genetics

Do I want to know if I have a genetic disorder?

Do I understand the genetic basis of my disease?

Do I understand the possible genetic basis of my partner's disease?

Do I want to undergo screening for genetic disorders?

Do I understand the risks involved in such screening?

What will I do when I know the results of the genetic screening?

Ante-Natal Care
What ante-natal care is available locally?

Do I need a scan or screening test?

Do I understand the nature and purpose of the scan or test?

What are the possible outcomes and which will I choose?

Giving Birth
Where do I want to have my baby?

What are the risks in having the baby at home as opposed to in a hospital?

What do the doctor and midwife advise?

Am I clear what the doctor and midwife's attitude is towards the birth process, natural childbirth, drugs, the use of forceps, Caesarean operations, epidurals, and cutting the wall of the vagina?

Have I explained what I want to happen?

Will my partner be present?

What advice have I been given about breast-feeding and resuming sexual intercourse?

Contraception
Do I want to use a contraceptive?

Do I understand the different forms of contraceptives and their disadvantages and risks?

If I am sterilised, do I understand the physical and psychological effects on me and my relationships?

Have I discussed matters of contraception or sterilisation with my partner?

Abortion
What is my attitude to my pregnancy?

Have I discussed the pregnancy with all those affected?

If I wish a termination, what are the grounds I will discuss with my doctor?

What is my doctor's attitude towards abortion?

If my doctor is opposed to abortion, where can I go for alternative advice?

Do I understand the risks and likely effects of abortion?

Do I understand the impact of my abortion on others?

What is my attitude towards when life begins?

Notes to Chapter 3

1. 'Report of the Committee of Inquiry into Human Fertilisation and Embryology', Cmnd 9314; The Committee on the Ethics of Gene Therapy under Sir C. Clothier (1992).

2. *R* v. *Ethical Committee of St Mary's Hospital*, ex p Harriott (1988) 1 FLR 512.

3. A family in Wisconsin had a child to provide bone marrow for another child who suffered from leukaemia.

4. Evidence given to the BMA Medical Ethics Committee suggested that information from other countries did not reveal a fall in the number of donors when identity was not kept secret.

5. The Department of Health Committee on the Ethics of Gene Therapy, 1989–1992, chaired by Sir C. Clothier; *see also* 'Our Genetic Future', *British Medical Journal* (1992).

6. 'Sex Selection', Human Fertilisation and Embryology Authority (HFEA) Public Consultation Document (January 1993).

7. Annual Report of the Chief Medical Officer, 1990.

8. *See* 'The Health of the Nation' (London, HMSO, 1992).

9. *Gillick* v. *Norfolk and Wisbech Area Health Authority and anor* (1985) 3 WLR 830, 3 AER 402 (1986) 1 A.C. (1986) Crim LR 113.

10. *See also D* v. *NSPCC* (1977) 1 A11 ER 589 (1978) A.C. 171.
11. Re B (A Minor) (Sterilisation) (1988) A.C. (1987) 2 A11 ER 206, HL. Re F (1990) 2 A.C. 1; *sub nom F* v. *West Berkshire Health Authority* (1989) 2 AER 545.
12. *Janaway* v. *Salford Health Authority* (1988) 3 AER 1079 HL.

4

CHOICE AND CHILDREN

As we grow and develop physically and psychologically from the baby state to full adulthood we are given more responsibility for ourselves. Children are treated differently from adults. We have different expectations about what children are able and allowed to do. Because we are concerned to protect children from themselves as well as from others, society takes responsibility for children in the home and at school. Such taking of responsibility is also true on the part of doctors when they have children as patients. If the basic model for the doctor–patient relationship is a partnership, then doctors and children are growing towards a partnership, where the child will take more responsibility for himself or herself as he or she matures.

The law has often tried to define the magic moment when children become adults and are considered sufficiently mature and legally responsible for themselves. Twenty-one was considered that coming of age, but in England it is now considered to be eighteen years. The young adult is then allowed to vote, fight for Queen and country and is held responsible for what he or she does. Yet the law is inconsistent. A child of sixteen is able to consent or refuse to have medical treatment, according to the Family Law Reform Act 1969. In Scotland, sixteen is the age of legal capacity and a recent Law Commission Report suggested that twelve was the age when society should presume a child was mature. The variety of figures shows the problems of trying to fix on one magic moment when the child becomes an adult. Rather, we are dealing with a process, which needs to recognise that maturity varies considerably both in children and adults. Children, like adults, may not even be consistent in expressing their ability to make their own decisions. We are able to cope less well at some times than at others. Emotional sways affect us all and our capacity to make rational decisions. If we do try to fasten on one specific age for becoming an adult, it might seem that anyone and everyone below that age is not to be consulted, for there is no competence or ability to make decisions. Such a view could be nonsense and bad medical practice. Doctors need to realise that all patients, but especially children, are individuals, whose competence and ability to decide comes and goes. The doctor must be sensitive to the child as a patient and try to involve the child as fully as possible in decisions about medical care and treatment.

One of the best descriptions of what is required of a child-patient in decision-making was set out in the Gillick judgement.[1] To take proper responsibility for medical decisions, a child must understand what is being proposed, the reasons for it and the likely consequences. The child must have enough ability to discriminate between different options to be able to make a wise decision. That wise decision should be in his or her own best interests. If a child is able to do this, then, regardless of age, he or she is considered competent and should be treated so by the doctor. As children move towards physical and mental maturity, they are regarded as increasingly competent and able to take responsibility for themselves. The child is then autonomous.

Limits of Autonomy

Autonomy is always limited in society. Even if all of us are able to think, and are competent to make decisions, act on them, cope with the consequences and able to relate to other people, society does not allow us to do anything and everything we wish. Our individual freedom is restricted by society to allow society to flourish and to maintain the freedoms of other people. The courts and doctors sometimes have to infringe on the rights and autonomy of some patients in their own best interests or those of society. Such limitations require careful medical justification by the doctor involved, but in no way affect the consistent medical responsibility to encourage every patient – child or adult – to make their own decisions and to use their capacities to the full.

The limiting of autonomy usually arises because of a conflict of interests. Such conflicts are all too common in families between parents and children. Parents often confirm that what their children want is certainly not what they as parents want. Parents and children may not only have different interests, they may also disagree fundamentally about what is in their best interests. That raises the question of who is to judge an individual's best interests. Doctors are often in the same situation as parents, where they may feel that a child-patient's best interests are not at all what the child regards them to be. Doctors must then balance respect for young people and their decisions with the need to protect them against harm from themselves and from others. Doctors also have a responsibility in the child-patient–doctor partnership to develop a child's capacity to make decisions and take increasing responsibility for his or her own health care.

The Basic Principles for Treating Children

In treating children, the same basic principles apply as to any and every patient. For the doctor, the patient comes first. When a child comes as a patient, the doctor should make sure that he or she is treating the child and not the parents. Some children suffer from Down's syndrome. They are not only mentally limited but their physical appearance is affected as well. Plastic surgery can change the facial characteristics of Down's syndrome sufferers and make them look 'normal'. Many parents are very keen to have their child operated on, especially if it is a girl, so that people will react more normally toward the child and not discriminate against him or her. Doctors are concerned that the motive for the operation may be more a matter of the inability or unwillingness of the parents to come to terms with the handicap of their child and a desire to appear as a 'normal' family. Such an operation might make the child more vulnerable, as people may make flawed judgements about the child's mental capacity and take advantage of the child. To justify putting a child through the pain of an operation, when he or she is unable to decide for him or herself, it must have an overwhelming gain for the child. For the doctor the interests of the child must come first.

Responsibility and competence

Doctors have an equal responsibility to inform and explain to a child as much as the child can grasp. This is not just important as a right of the child, but will develop a pattern of how the child and doctor relate to each other. Children should know what is happening to them and why it is being done. Their wishes and consent should be gained for the simplest procedure. This has some limits. No child is going to be keen to have an injection, even if it will be a benefit in the long run. Perhaps adults are really no different here. Screaming children will still require an injection if it is genuinely necessary. Doctors and parents should do all they can to calm the child and reason with him or her. There are some excellent children's books available which show what happens when we go to the doctor's and explain in simple language and pictures so a child can grasp what is going on.

As patients we are assumed to be competent. In the case of children, doctors do have to make hard decisions about their competence. There is no absolute definition or standard and no guaranteed way of reaching such a standard. Inevitably, doctors recognise the individual variations of patients and the different capacities all of us have at different times. Children's competence does not just depend on their intelligence and ability. It also depends on how society treats them and the expectations we have of children. If we think a child is able to act responsibly, then that child often does. The opposite is also the case. Such experience should encourage doctors to give children as much responsibility as possible. In the British Medical Association Medical Ethics Handbook Working Party, there was startling evidence presented by doctors working with seriously ill children. They introduced the notion of 'wisdom' rather than just knowledge. Often a seriously ill child grasps what is involved in future treatment because of past experience. A child in such circumstances may have an uncanny degree of perception and insight and a healthy ability to imagine what will happen to him or her. When it comes to treatment designed to prevent disease it is harder for a child to understand fully the implications of what might and might not happen. Even if children are not able to make major decisions about things like operations, they can still be involved by asking if they have any questions and if they would like their parents to help. Doctors need to encourage and to take seriously the confidence of children where appropriate. Children have the right to be thoroughly involved in decisions about themselves. If they have sufficient understanding and are able to make correct assessments and interpretations, then they are just as competent as many adults.

The child's best interests

Doctors are in the business of acting in the best interests of the patient. The child as patient's welfare comes first. When a child expresses what he or she wants and makes a decision, doctors must ask whether or not it is genuinely in the child's best interests. Normally this means that medical treatment should be given whenever the advantages outweigh the disadvantages. Such decisions will mean careful consideration of the quality of life of the child before, during and after treatment. Part of a proper competence is the ability to make decisions in the light of our best interests. If children make decisions that are clearly against their own best interests, then they are regarded as incompetent. What most people would do in the same circumstances is a valid way of assessing what counts as best interests. Whatever an adult – whether this is a doctor or a parent – decides on behalf of a child, that decision must be checked and scrutinised. Adults can make bad decisions just as easily as children. Doctors must not force their practices and wishes on a child-patient, any more than a parent is entitled to do so. Doctors must seek to persuade and to help children grasp why their wishes are being overridden concerning a particular treatment.

The children of today are the patients not just of the here and now but also of tomorrow. How doctors relate to and treat children will have a great impact on how these children will view doctors when they become adults. The doctors must encourage the child to make as many decisions as possible and to be involved in all decision-making. The doctor should encourage the moves to greater competence on the part of the child. Likewise, doctors should encourage the child to communicate with parents and families. In the difficult cases, like over contraception, doctors must not breach the confidentiality of the patient. The doctor should encourage the young person to consult with parents, as far as possible. As part of the move to a genuine partnership between doctors and patients, doctors must foster trust and confidence. Through these measures children can be encouraged to have more confidence in doctors.

Conflict with parents

If doctors are required to act in the best interests of a child, they also have a duty to prevent harm. The protection of children is a serious concern for society. When children are vulnerable and at risk because of immaturity, weakness or inexperience, society in general and doctors in particular have a greater responsibility for preserving the well-being and safety of the child. If a child makes a decision which will lead to serious and irreparable harm, the doctor must override that decision to prevent harm. If parents make decisions about what should or should not happen to their children, doctors may have to have these set aside. Such a step involves seeking legal support and a decision to overturn the wishes of parents. Whenever there is an irreversible decision about what will happen to someone, like a child who is unable to give consent, the courts must be consulted. This will cover cases like the children of Jehovah's Witnesses refusing blood transfusions, sterilisation, and tissue or organ donation. The medical bias is usually in favour of treatment rather than not to treat. This can lead to conflict with parents, who may wish medicine to stop trying and thus to allow their child to die. This is extremely harrowing for all concerned, but the doctor retains a responsibility for the child, and if there is a sound clinical judgement that life should be preserved and some genuine quality of life maintained, then the courts will have to be involved. In such cases, it is likely that the doctors will be supported in the best interests of the child and to protect the child from harm. In cases of abuse, doctors will be concerned to preserve the integrity and well-being of the child. This may involve taking legal steps to ensure the child's safety and protection. In all situations where children and parents disagree the doctor will try to act as an honest broker. If that fails, then the courts must be consulted.

Competing Claims

In a society where the notion of rights is widely discussed, there may arise competing claims and conflicts between the rights of the child and the rights of the parent. As children are seen increasingly as people in their own right, autonomous and free to make their own decisions, some parents are concerned about the erosion of parental rights. Parents argue that they are responsible for their children not just in material ways, but also for their emotional and psychological well-being. They are also legally responsible for the damage done by their children, if the child breaks the law. Parents claim that they not only know their child, but also that they are in the best position to make judgements about the child's future and best interests.

The Children Act 1989 sets out the way children should be involved in decisions about their welfare and health. Problems may arise when a child refuses a specific treatment which the doctor regards as being in the child's best interests. It seems that the law requires more of children when they refuse treatment than when they give consent to that treatment. It is almost as if children are free to give consent, but not to refuse treatment. This is certainly the case in life-threatening situations. Doctors will have to try to assess the reasons for a child's refusal of treatment. As with all of us when refusing treatment, the doctor will consider how competent we are to make such a decision, whether it is a consistent and well-established decision, whether we do actually understand the consequences of our decision and what most people would do if they were in our position. Usually, the standard is expressed as what a wise and prudent person would choose. All of these judgements mean that doctors must communicate clearly with the individual patient at every level and encourage the child's participation in the decision-making process.

Who gives consent?

For any patient, including children, valid consent assumes not just the giving of relevant information about treatment options, but also the ability to make decisions. Competence involves understanding the choices at stake and the consequences of those choices. We as patients need to grasp the reasons for treatment, its nature, any side-effects, and the likely outcome of such treatment. We need to know what alternatives there are to that treatment. We also need to be free from pressure and willing and able to give a rational decision. Adult patients are able to refuse treatment even though it may be in their own best interests to have it. Children are not given such rights if there is serious risk of harm to them. There seems to be a different level of competence required in order to refuse something from what is necessary to give consent. The more serious the results of the decision to refuse treatment, the greater awareness there must be of what that refusal means.[2] In situations of doubt, the courts will have to be involved and take both the decision and the responsibility for the results into account.

If children as patients are competent to understand treatment options and their consequences, then they are able to give valid consent. It is generally wise for parents to be involved in such decisions, especially if the results could have serious consequences for the young person. Doctors must try to encourage open and frank discussion between children and parents, but if that is impossible and the child is competent, then the doctor must act on the consent of the child-patient, even when it may conflict with the parents' wishes. Parents do not own their children. If the child wishes his or her medical contract with the doctor to be private and confidential, the doctor should honour that wish.

Where children are not competent, either because of their age and stage of development, or because of their illness, then parents are able to decide for the child. In cases of conflict between parents, or if there is an unmarried mother, the woman is assumed to have the final authority. Ideally, couples will discuss any treatment options and be able to come to an agreement. If divorced or separated, both parents may share responsibility and should both be consulted, especially if the medical matter is serious. We have already seen that if parents make bad choices for their children, doctors can override that choice if their action is clearly in the best interests of the child. If necessary, the courts need to be consulted to approve the doctor's decision and action.

The severely malformed baby

In cases of a severely malformed baby, the doctor is responsible for the well-being of the child. Before undertaking necessary steps to preserve the life of a malformed baby where that life is threatened, there should be discussion with the parents. Even though this is an extremely painful and stressful time and the parents may be in a state of shock, it is vital that they are helped to understand the situation, what is happening and will happen to their baby and then involved in the final decision to begin treatment or to withhold it. The doctor must not force parents to carry a load of responsibility they are unable or unwilling to take. They should be given sensitive advice and encouragement to consult others who the parents may trust and feel will help them. The patient is the sick child, but the doctor also has responsibility for the parent and the wider family members.

In an emergency, doctors must act to preserve life. However, decisions about treating severely handicapped babies are not always urgent. Doctors should allow as much time as possible to permit parents to come to terms with the awful reality and to think through the short- and long-term consequences of their decision. Parents are always free to change their minds, but doctors need to recognise that this might only be a stage in the decision process.

If, together, a decision is made not to treat or continue medical treatment, the usual love and care must be given to the child. All staff should understand what is happening and why that decision has been made. The comfort of both the child and the parents is a primary concern. These decisions involve hard judgements about quality of life and the painful results of medical treatment often over a long period of time. If there is any prospect of some serious quality of life and any benefit from a medical treatment, the child should not be deprived of that benefit and life, even if the parents prefer such treatment to be rejected. There is no justification for any general withholding of treatment from children solely on the grounds that they are handicapped. The normal and basic pre-supposition is that human life is to be preserved, and only in exceptional settings where there is no real quality of life are the courts likely to support the withdrawal or withholding of treatment.

Abuse, Visual Material and Consent

In the case of abuse, visual evidence may be vital. Doctors should, as always, involve the child in a decision to take a photograph or videotape. The same holds true if visual material is taken for clinical reasons, for example to chart the progress of a disease or of treatment. If the police are involved, they are responsible for taking any visual material. If it is for a clinical reason, then the doctor can and should control what happens. Problems may arise if the child refuses to be photographed. To avoid further danger to the child, such material should not be recorded unless it is required for criminal proceedings or to help with necessary treatment for the child or other family members. Such cases are thankfully exceptional and the emphasis should be in making sure that such steps are in the child's best interests. Child-patients have the right to have their privacy protected and confidentiality maintained. This applies to their medical records and to any visual material. When they are old enough to make their own decisions, they should be consulted to ensure they are willing to have visual material about them used in areas like research or teaching. There are a number of registered medical illustrators who can be used in collecting visual material. They follow a strict code of practice and will safeguard the anonymity and confidentiality of the child. Always the stress on the part of the doctor should be on making sure, as carefully and thoroughly as possible, that consent has been given and confidentiality is assured.

Children and Confidentiality

Children as patients enjoy the same confidentiality as the rest of us in medical matters. If a child is able to understand the significance of a medical record, he or she has the right to consult that record and is free to forbid other people from that access. That includes parents. Private information may not be given to anyone else unless there is some vital issue involving the health and safety of someone else or it is clearly in the best interests of the child. Parents have no automatic rights to confidential medical information about their children if the children are competent and refuse to allow their parents access. Even if the child is not competent to make a decision about a treatment or about the notes, if a doctor is sure that the child-patient would not want something to be revealed and the child thought that what was discussed was private, then the doctor must respect the child's confidentiality.

Problems do arise if it would be in the best interests of a child that certain confidential information was known, as in cases of child abuse. Children must be protected from abuses and the necessary information should only be given to the relevant authorities. A doctor who is treating a child who does not want anyone to know about the abuse, must be totally convinced it is really in the child's best interests to keep such information confidential. In the setting of a case conference with other professionals like social workers and teachers, doctors are often concerned that different standards of confidentiality are at work and different responsibilities to those in authority. Doctors should then only disclose what is necessary. It would be best if those concerns over confidentiality were aired and some general agreement reached and observed. In the case of highly sensitive material, a doctor may ask for a private hearing or give written advice for the eyes of the chair only. The consent of the child should be obtained whenever possible, but the central focus, as always, in the treatment and care of children must be on what is best for the child.

Children and Research

The use of children in research is sometimes unavoidable. Adults are normally able to consent and be involved in research projects, but information on and understanding of childhood illnesses may necessarily involve research with children. Hopefully, such research will have some direct benefit for the child concerned, but it may only have a longer term benefit for others. If children are competent to make decisions about themselves and their own treatment then they are quite capable of deciding whether or not to take part in research. Doctors conduct research not simply to benefit patients but also to test new treatments. If the answer was already known and all the risks clear, there would be no need for research. It is precisely to gather such information that research takes place. If children are competent, they can decide to take part in research which will benefit them directly. If a child is not able to make such a decision, then parents can. Researchers should try to encourage competent children to discuss the research project and their involvement with their parents and gain their approval. While no one would object to the simple gathering of facts and statistics in order to understand the progress and spread of a childhood disease, research which has no benefit for a child is much harder to justify. If a child can understand the point and any risks involved in the research, then consent can be given by the child.

All these details should have been approved by and checked with the Local Research Ethics Committee. It is their job to make sure that the rights of any child-patient are properly protected in any research. LRECs will forbid research involving actions which will do harm to a child or his or her interests. It may allow research if there is only a minimal risk and no foreseen harm to the child. The consent of the child – if possible – and parents must be forthcoming.

Causing a child pain

Doctors involved in research should try to make sure that they are not simply duplicating work already done and so causing unnecessary pain to children. Parents are sometimes under pressure to allow their children to take part in research projects. Researchers need to be aware of the way they might put inappropriate pressure on parents and where such parents might not understand the nature of the research and also feel unable to refuse.[3] As the research proceeds, doctors need to be vigilant for signs of any negative responses or signs that the child is being affected. As with all medicine, the key is the partnership between doctors and child-patients. Parents may also have a role in this partnership, but the primary concern for the doctor must be the well-being of the child.

It is unusual for children to be used as live donors in transplantation. Such a donation may be able to save the life of a brother or sister, and some would feel that a child donor might benefit from knowing that they played a vital role. It is normally considered unethical to use organs or tissue from people who are unable to give valid consent. If a child is considered competent and able to make such a decision in a desperate situation, doctors must do all they can to make sure that there is genuine understanding of all that is involved and that there is no improper pressure from parents or family to force a child to donate. This kind of donation should only arise for the direct benefit of a family member and as a last resort.

Children and the Law

Adulthood is attained in law in England and Wales at eighteen, according to the Family Law Reform Act 1969, and in Scotland at sixteen, according to the Age of Legal Capacity (Scotland) Act

1991. In the case of medical care and treatment a sixteen-year-old can give consent and choose a doctor without consulting parents. Parental rights remain as long as they are needed for the protection of the child, but these must yield to the child's own decision, as long as the child has sufficient understanding and intelligence to make a proper decision.[4] The nature of the sharing of responsibilities between parents and children is set out in the Children Act 1989. Lord Donaldson held that there was a difference between consenting and withholding consent to treatment.[5] The clinical judgement of the doctor remains intact in such cases. Emergency treatment for children is unlikely to lead to any risk to a doctor from the courts.[6] The involvement of children in consenting to take part in research is covered by advice from the Medical Research Council, December 1991, 'The Ethical Conduct of Research on Children' and the General Medical Council's 'Guidance for Doctors on Professional Confidence', November 1991 and advice from the Department of Health. The Gillick case set in law the right of a child under sixteen to have contraceptive advice and treatment without parental knowledge and consent, if the young person has sufficient understanding and intelligence. The GMC advice differs from that of the BMA and allows doctors discretion to inform parents if that decision can be justified and the young person is informed. (See Department of Health 'Guidelines for Local Research Ethics Committees'.)

The Child-Patient–Doctor Relationship

A genuine partnership involves careful listening and responding to the other person's needs. Young people do not always feel that their GP will take the time to listen properly and may worry that their confidentiality may be broken. Doctors must make it clearer to children and young people that they are willing to listen and what they hear and learn will be kept confidential. Help lines, radio and television doctors and those who write medical columns in magazines have a very special responsibility towards those who call up, listen to or read what they say. Such doctors are only able to give general advice and should always encourage the young person to consult the local GP, who will know the child-patient and their history and background.

Children are vulnerable and yet are growing into full maturity. Doctors must balance the protection of the child with allowing maximum choice and responsibility. All of us learn how to choose by making our own decisions and living with the consequences. Doctors must help children to do that, protecting them only from serious harm. Doctors have duties to the parents of children, but must not allow these responsibilities to interfere with proper care of the child. Only where there is a risk to the child or to others should doctors breach confidentiality. Such exceptions do not detract from the general rule that children are encouraged to make their own choices, in the knowledge and security that doctors will protect them from harm and keep confidential whatever the child wishes to remain private. This is the pattern for a good partnership today and will build secure doctor–patient relationships in the future.

Questions about Children

Do I understand what the doctor is explaining to me?

What do I think about the treatment the doctor wants me to have?

What do my parents think about the treatment the doctor wants me to have?

Am I able to discuss this with them?

Have I tried to help them understand what I want and feel?

Is there someone else who could help me to communicate better with them?

Do I understand what the doctor's attitude is towards my confidentiality?

Do I understand why the doctor thinks I should discuss this with my parents?

Do I want my parents to know and be involved?

Notes to Chapter 4
1. *Gillick* v. *Norfolk and Wisbech Area Health Authority and anor* (1985) 3 WLR 830, 3 AER 402 (1986) 1 A.C. (1986) Crim LR 113.
2. Re F (1990) 2 A.C.; *sub nom F* v. *West Berkshire Health Authority* (1989) 2 AER 545.
3. *British Medical Journal*, 300 (26 May 1990), 372–5; *see also* R.H. Nicholson (ed.) *Medical Research with Children* (OUP, 1986).
4. *Gillick, op. cit.*
5. Re R (A Minor) (Wardship: medical treatment) (1991) 4 AER 177.
6. NHS Circular HSC (Gen) 81 (1975).
7. 'The Ethical Conduct of Research on Children', Medical Research Council, December 1991.

5

TREATMENT AND PRESCRIBING

Many of the other chapters in this book deal directly with specific issues of treatment, non-treatment and prescribing. If the reader needs help on a particular problem, the relevant chapter should be consulted. While it is not possible to cover every specific treatment issue, there are important general things which we need to know in order to make proper choices. These principles apply in all but the most extreme cases. The aim of this chapter will be to focus on the principles which undergird all decisions about treatment and prescribing.

We as patients consult doctors because we have medical needs. Doctors are providing a service to meet those needs and to act in the best interests of each of us as patients. Needs are not the same as wants and desires and the importance of this distinction will be discussed in the Chapter on Resource Allocation. Doctors are obliged to meet genuine medical needs whenever possible. They are never obliged to give us all we want. Wanting not only does not get, but should not. Doctors need to differentiate between what we as patients want and need very carefully. They should also ensure that there is a genuine medical need and it is possible and proper to treat that need. To offer and provide such treatment must always be subject to the patient's explicit consent. We as patients should understand what the treatment entails and must give fully informed valid consent before doctors treat us or prescribe for us. Such consent is only possible where and when there has been a full discussion and explanation, and genuine understanding on our part. The doctor must also be convinced that the particular treatment will do its job properly and is appropriate.

Effective Treatment

Medicine is a science as well as an art. Over time, we find that different drugs and treatments produce very different results. We then have to check the reliability of these drugs, treatments and their effects to see which are the most effective. The technical literature in medicine is full of the results of such scientific testing and research. Part of the work of doctors is to improve the effectiveness of different drugs and treatments. Only if there is objective, reliable data can proper decisions be made and the best and most effective treatments be used in any particular case. Being a doctor is a bit like being a detective. From the clues patients give in describing their symptoms and as a result of examinations and clinical tests, the doctor forms a theory about what is wrong. The doctor makes a diagnosis based on the evidence before him or her and from years of experienced training. However, diagnosis is only part of the doctor's job. The doctor has then to decide what will be the most effective and appropriate response and treatment options. All of this should be explained to us as the patient, not just at the end, but all the way along, so we know what is happening and are involved in understanding the decisions and choice we will make together with the doctor.

The doctor provides the diagnosis and describes the treatment options available and their different degrees of effectiveness. Doctors have sometimes been guilty of giving drugs which have no real effect or benefit for the patient. They have a moral and clinical responsibility to ensure that they are up to date with current scientific assessment of the success of different treatments and the likely side-effects. All of this information should be explained to us as patients, to allow us to make a fully informed choice. Sometimes we can view doctors almost like a witch doctor. Even when some of us are given drugs which are known to be harmless and ineffective, we still get better. This is called the placebo effect. It is not good medical practice to give patients unnecessary and ineffective drugs simply to make us 'feel' better. This would be more psychology than medicine. It involves the manipulation of patients by doctors, who are only pretending to give genuine treatment. Even though there might be an actual physical and psychological benefit for an individual patient, such pretence destroys the honesty and integrity of the doctor's partnership with us as patients. To justify such a procedure it would have to be clearly a last resort and categorically in our best interests. Normally speaking, all of us as patients should only be given drugs and treatment because these are genuinely going to make a difference and lead to the improvement or relief of symptoms and pain.

Appropriate Treatment

There can be pressure on doctors simply to give something. Some patients often seem to think that the only good doctor is one who writes a prescription. Often a consultation with the doctor will begin with a patient saying, 'Please give me something for . . .' It is all too easy for a doctor to give in to our demands, especially if the doctor is busy, under pressure, or if we are a difficult person. It is also wrong for a doctor to give in without a careful assessment of the genuine need for that treatment. They must ask whether treatment is appropriate for us in a particular set of circumstances.

To discover how appropriate treatment will be, the doctor will have to take the time to get to the actual problem and its causes. One danger in all medicine is that of treating the symptoms and not dealing with the underlying causes. Part of assessing what is appropriate is taking time to listen to what we are really asking and saying. The first question people ask may not be the actual question to which they want to know the answer, and inappropriate treatment would be the wrong response. A woman who was newly diagnosed as having motor neurone disease, which is a particularly nasty degenerative disease, did not understand what it meant. She asked her doctor what would happen to her. He told her she would choke to death. She then suffered months of nightmares, imagining that she was choking to death. What she really wanted to know was the next stage of the disease and her degeneration. More time and sensitivity on the part of the doctor would have made sure of the question as well as ensuring an appropriate answer given in a more careful and constructive manner.

Cost-Effective Treatment

Everything has a price and as the costs of medicines and treatments spiral, doctors are having to make decisions which have financial implications. The aim in the National Health Service has been to give us as patients what we need. This is now being scrutinised in light of costs. To treat one patient with an expensive drug is to deprive another patient of treatment. One answer is to give more money; then everyone would get the treatment needed, regardless of cost. In a time of recession, this will not happen. Doctors do have to consider the cost implications of treatment. This does not mean depriving patients of what is genuinely needed. It does mean exploring more economic drug and treatment options. Doctors have a responsibility to us as their patients to give the best treatment we as a society can afford. As patients we have a responsibility to be sensible in what we can expect. Where doctors and patients have the choice of cheaper treatments which are equally effective, there is a moral responsibility to other patients to be economical. These issues are dealt with more fully in the Chapter on Resource Allocation.

There is another dimension to the financial concerns in treatment decisions. Doctors can and do make money from medicine and from drugs. Drug companies offer incentives to doctors if they are willing to prescribe the company's drugs to patients. While there are strict rules about payment for such treatments, there may be other incentives offered as inducements. We as patients need to be assured that doctors are giving drugs and treatment in our best interests and not because of incentives from drug companies.

Safe Treatment

When oral contraceptives were first prescribed for women, doctors assumed that there were no major risks. There were some side-effects, which put a number of women off using the Pill. It was only over a long period of time that researchers discovered that certain kinds of contraceptive pills could cause heart disease. These were then withdrawn. There is a Committee for the Safety of Drugs which gives a licence for the use of new medicines. Before such a licence is granted, the evidence must indicate that the drug is safe and that the side-effects are minimal or can be fairly easily controlled. It is only in desperate situations where there is no other alternative that the use of untested drugs might be permitted. Medicines can harm us. Too much taken over too long a period of time can lead to abuse and dependency, as well as physical and psychological harm. My own mother became dependent on sleeping pills, after a bereavement, and was unable to break the habit. Government attention has focused on the cost of over-prescribing but, from the patient's point of view, safety is much more important. If drugs are dangerous they must be given only for a short period of time to deal with the particular problems requiring treatment. Dependency should be avoided. The danger of someone using a large quantity of drugs to take his or her own life must be carefully monitored if the patient is vulnerable and at risk. Doctors should not only be concerned about the safety of the drug or treatment itself, but of possible abuses by patients and the risk of long-term dependency.

Obviously, doctors can only be held responsible for the foreseeable and avoidable consequences of treatment. In Edinburgh, there was extensive use of a new treatment for cancer. Early results indicated that the treatment was highly successful because there were no repeat cancers among patients. The problem was only discovered much later.[1] There was no repeat cancer because the patients were dead. Doctors do not have any way of guaranteeing what will happen in the future. New drugs and treatments may eventually be found to have harmful results. Doctors are responsible for acting on the evidence they have. They are also morally and clinically obliged to keep abreast of new evidence and continuing assessments of treatments. Patient safety requires regular checking. While it may be much more convenient to sign a prescription form left in the GP's office, doctors need to ensure a regular follow-up of all patients who are on long-term medication. This again will prevent the wrong kind of dependency and abuse. If there are safety risks to us as patients there is all the more need to discuss this with us. We are the ones who must accept the risk and live with the consequences. Our choice as patient is crucial in all treatment decisions. It is especially important if there is any degree of risk or likely side-effects involved. We are responsible for our own bodies. What is done to them should remain our choice and no one else's.

Information about Treatments and Drugs

For us as patients to make proper decisions about treatment or medicine, we need to be informed about that treatment – its nature, side-effects, purpose and likely consequences. Any risks involved in such treatment should be spelled out. If there are alternative medicines or treatments available, we have the right to know about these and why the doctor recommends the particular option he or she does. Doctors will vary over how far they should go in describing the risks of treatments with us. They would also debate over how much detail should be covered about possible complications, especially if these are extremely unlikely. As a rough guide, doctors tend to point out any risk beyond two or three per cent. If it is less, most doctors would not regard that as statistically very significant. However, to the one in fifty patients who are affected, this complication or risk is an actuality and very important. At its extreme, as in the United States, patients have the right to know every possible risk, however unlikely and bizarre. If they are not given that detail and something does go wrong, then they will sue the doctor. Doctors and patients in the United Kingdom have resisted this contract basis for medicine and tried to prevent a slide towards defensive medicine where the doctor treats patients simply to defend himself or herself from legal claims rather than in our best interests. Many doctors feel that most of us patients do not want to know all the possible nasty things that might happen. We do want to know the general risks.[2] However, we might be harmed and become more anxious if we are told of extremely unlikely scenarios. It might actually affect our rate of recovery and attitude towards treatment.

While patients may not have an absolute right or need to know every last risk, we do have a right to know that risk if that is our wish. As patients we must be treated as the adults we are. If we want to have a fully informed choice and to have all the details of treatment options and risks, then we will have to cope with that knowledge and choice and its impact on us. In other words, doctors must not mislead or refuse to give information which is relevant to the patient's decision-making process. The good doctor will explore with us how much is genuinely desired to be known and act accordingly. Where we have preferences over treatment forms, as in contraceptive practices or possible damage to a fetus during a pregnancy, those preferences should be respected by the doctor. If we as patients are to co-operate in partnership with doctors, good levels of information will ensure that partnership works well.

Doctors' Prescribing Responsibilities

When a doctor writes a prescription he or she is responsible for what is prescribed. As with lawyers, doctors' choices of treatments and drugs must not just be made on a proper professional basis, but must also be seen to be so made, according to the General Medical Services Committee in the *British Medical Journal*, May 1988. The doctor is responsible for maintaining the best interests of the patient in light of limited medical resources. The prescription of medicines, however, is not just left to the doctor alone. It is the taxpayer, through the National Health Service, who pays for drugs. The Government has therefore a proper concern to make sure that our money is being spent well and wisely. A whole battery of audit measures and reviews of prescribing habits has led to increasing education and guidance for doctors. It is important that individual doctors understand the trends and patterns in their own prescribing behaviour. Such information can provide a useful tool for correction and for future planning. It also gives a basis for sound medical teaching. Each month GPs receive information about their prescribing amounts and the impact this will have on doctors' budgets.

Unfortunately, this kind of information can work to the detriment of some patients. The chronically and long-term sick or those who require expensive drugs can be disproportionately expensive, not just in financial treatment and prescription costs, but also in time and care. Some doctors could use the budgeting information as a basis for getting rid of such expensive patients. The General Medical Council has taken a strong line on any such discriminating moves. In the GMC Guidelines issued in November 1991, they state that, '. . . it is unacceptable to abuse the right to refuse to accept patients by applying criteria of access to the practice list which discriminate against groups of patients on the grounds of their age, sex, sexual orientation, race, colour, religious belief, perceived economic worth or the amount of work they are likely to generate by virtue of their clinical condition.' This makes quite clear the moral limits to a doctor's prescribing freedom.

Conflicts over who pays for treatment and prescriptions have increased since the purchaser–provider pattern was introduced. Now that GP budgets are capped, GPs may refuse to pay for expensive hospital treatment if the patient is no longer their patient but 'belongs' to a consultant. Patients ought not to be allowed to suffer in such cases and should refer to the local Family Health Services Authority.

Patients' Interests

Before prescribing treatment or drugs, the doctor must use established wisdom and guidelines. Medical literature and colleagues provide such information. We as patients will need to be involved in the discussion of different options and their likely results, and aware of any financial implications. If we have a preference and choose one drug or treatment rather than another, the doctor will need to know why that choice has been made. If such a preference costs much more and there are cheaper, equally effective, alternatives, then the doctor's obligation is not just to us, but to all the other patients who will be affected and may be deprived of treatment as a result of this choice. One patient's choice cannot justify the exclusion and harm of other patients and the removal of their choices. The doctor will need to share the dilemma with us. We as patients must not be shielded from the harsh realisation of resource allocation. The doctor should provide us with an objective judgement about the most effective and appropriate treatment or drug, based on experience and knowledge.

An interesting shift is happening in the interests of the patient and in the development of the doctor–patient partnership. General practices are offering regular check-ups and providing new services like 'Well Woman Clinics'. These are seeking to educate all of us as patients into taking more responsibility for our health and to prevent heart disease, avoid cancer and the like. Smears, cholesterol-level testing, diet, weight and blood pressure checks all indicate when problems may arise and ways to prevent such problems should be sought. All of us must take full advantage of such services.

In a similar way, the provision of immunisation and vaccination for children is clearly a way of preventing disease and protecting patients from whooping cough, diphtheria, smallpox, measles and polio. It is in the interests of all of us as patients to use these prevention treatments as a largely safe way of health care. Flu jabs and regular tetanus boosters are another example of protection for patients. Early action, with minor inconveniences, can prevent serious problems in health care. Doctors are increasingly offering guidance about the availability of diagnostic procedures and preventive treatments. This is not just good for us as individuals. It is also vital for the health of the nation. It will reap tremendous benefits, as the money saved by not having to treat many of these diseases can be reallocated to other non-preventable diseases. Health education is the responsibility of doctors and patients. More and more through schools and public advertising patients and prospective patients are being better informed about the need to eat and exercise properly and to take simple precautions to enhance our health and avoid disease and the need for medical treatment.

Patient Pressure

The doctor–patient partnership does not extend to giving us everything we want. We may think we need a drug, when the doctor is medically convinced that it is unnecessary. It may also be harmful and create dependency. Sleeping pills and various drugs which help in slimming are often demanded by patients, even when doctors explain the risk of abuse and dependency. The doctor will need to be sensitive and ensure that as patients we are properly listened to and have a chance to explain why we feel as we do. The doctor must also explain his or her position and the reasoning behind it. If the doctor is unable to persuade us to do without a particular drug or to accept a cheaper or less dependency-creating alternative, he or she is neither clinically nor morally justified in prescribing what we want when it goes against a considered clinical judgement. Doctors are not required to do anything and everything patients want. In that sense, our choice as patients is limited. Such limits are a necessary and proper part of the doctor–patient partnership.

When Different Doctors are Involved

The more doctors specialise, the more different doctors will be responsible for different aspects of our care and treatment as patients. Good communication is vital between doctors to avoid mistakes and to prevent drugs and treatment working against each other and producing yet more problems for the patient. Ideally, one doctor should be in charge of a patient's total care and treatment package. As in nursing settings, there has been a move to particular nurses taking responsibility for an individual patient's nursing care. The same could and should be true for doctors. Hospital doctors and GPs need to be clear who is responsible for prescribing needs and paying for such treatment costs. This can create particular problems, where private doctors suggest that a GP prescribe treatment on the NHS. It is hard to argue that a GP can in any way be held responsible for treatment or prescriptions which in no way stem from his or her contact with a particular patient. Doctors need to be clear with each other about who has ultimate responsibility for prescribing and when that responsibility is given to another doctor. An example is when a patient leaves hospital to go home. It is advised that the hospital provide the necessary drugs for at least seven days. That leaves good time for the GP to be informed of the hospital's diagnosis, treatment and prescription decisions. GPs need to understand why such drugs have been prescribed as they take over responsibility for prescribing them. The person who writes the prescription is responsible for what is prescribed, in accordance with the Medicines Act 1968.

More difficult issues arise when patients consult doctors privately in clinics which specialise in sexual problems, hair or weight loss. Often such clinics do not liaise with the GP about the specific needs and risks of a patient. Appetite suppressants have been found to create such risks that they should not be used.[3] Doctors who work in such clinics must accept clinical responsibility for the advice they give. They should encourage the patients to allow contact with the GP. They should make absolutely clear the risks and limitations of particular drugs and treatments. The prescribing of drugs rests in the hands of doctors, who must accept responsibility for what is prescribed and its administration to the patient.

When Non-Medics are Involved

The relationship between doctors and nurses has not always been very harmonious. With continued professionalisation and rising academic standards in nursing, senior nurses are increasingly being given wider responsibilities. This includes the freedom and right to prescribe drugs and treatments, for which the nurse is clinically responsible, as stated in the Medicinal Products: Prescription by Nurses, etc. Act 1992. Good communication between nurses and doctors must be maintained to prevent confusion over treatment. Doctors are already benefiting from the time saved by such practical help, which still provides excellent care for the patient's treatment needs.

With alternative therapies, the treatments and products do not usually require a prescription. While doctors may doubt the scientific validity and practical results of complementary medicine, it is unlikely that it will interfere with a doctor's prescribing role. We as patients are increasingly voting with our feet and consulting alternative practitioners. Some of the issues raised are discussed on page 184. Doctors themselves are increasingly involving other forms of therapy like hypnotherapy or acupuncture. When this happens, the medical doctor retains clinical responsibility for the patient.

Drug Abuse

The picture most of us have of drug abuse is of young people and folk on the fringes of society. The reality is that drug problems are growing not just among such groups, but also in what is considered 'mainstream' society. It is legal for addicts to be given appropriate drug support in caring for them.[4] Doctors are advised to try to avoid creating dependency by being careful in the use of drugs and only prescribing such high-risk drugs when absolutely necessary. Drug dependency may simply be a habit of taking pills, which may have little positive or negative effect but which do provide the patient with some sense of psychological security. Doctors must care for those who are dependent on drugs. Such drug dependency can create a tremendous strain on the doctor–patient relationship. More effort will be required of the doctor to cope with such patients and try to maintain the partnership.

Legal Responsibilities

A doctor is only required to do what is reasonably expected and appropriate. Patients cannot sue a doctor for negligence unless there is a clear failure to use reasonable care which results in damage to someone. According to the Bolam judgement the standards expected and required of doctors are what a reasonably skilled and experienced doctor would ordinarily use.[5] According to the Limitation Act 1980, legal actions may only be brought within three years of an injury or death, unless new information becomes available. The rules for allowing the disclosure of medical records are set out in the Supreme Court Act of 1981. The freedom of junior doctors and medical students is tightly controlled by more senior doctors being responsible for them.[6] NHS regulations state that GPs have a legal duty to refer their NHS patients to specialists.[7]

When making complaints against doctors, two different sets of rules apply. Complaints against a GP should be made to the Family Health Services Authority. Complaints against hospital doctors should be made to the hospital, according to the Hospital Complaints Procedures Act 1985. If a patient needs help or is dissatisfied, then the Community Health Council and the Health Service Commissioner (a kind of ombudsman) may be consulted. Direct complaints to the GMC are also available for both categories of doctors, but these would be sent to the appropriate bodies first. How doctors are controlled in their dealings with drugs is clearly set out in 'Rights and Responsibilities of Doctors', *British Medical Journal* (1992).

In conclusion, doctors' skill and medical expertise lies not just in diagnosis but in treatment. The whole battery of drugs and therapies available could totally confuse a patient. In the partnership between doctors and patients, the doctor's task is to guide us through the maze of treatment options. Guidance and direction must never take the place of informed consent and patient choice. Good prescribing and treatment will maintain the sense of trust in the partnership.

Questions about Treatment and Prescribing

Has the doctor explained why I need this treatment or prescription?

Has the doctor explained the likely effects of this on me?

Has the doctor explained any risks of the treatment?

Has the doctor explained what will happen if I don't have this treatment?

Has the doctor offered and explained any alternative forms of treatment?

Am I clear why the doctor recommends this particular treatment rather than the others?

Have I given proper consent for the treatment to begin and to continue?

Am I aware of the cost implications of this treatment, if these affect other people?

Notes to Chapter 5
1. Conference of the Scottish Radiological Society, lecture on the Cyclotron Unit by Prof. D. Forrester.
2. This may be necessary to protect a doctor in law. *See* 'Rights and Responsibilities of Doctors', *British Medical Journal* (1992), 22–4 and 131–4.
3. *See* 'Medical Ethics Today: its practice and philosophy', *British Medical Journal* (1993).
4. Misuse of Drugs (Notification of, and Supply to Addicts) Regulations (SI 1973 No. 799).
5. *Bolam* v. *Friern Barnet Hospital HMC* (1957) 2 AER 118, 1 WLR 582.
6. *Wilsher* v. *Essex Area Health Authority* (1987) 2 WLR 425; *see also* Medical Act 1956, 1978, 1983.
7. NHS (General Medical and Pharmaceutical Services) Regulations (SI 1974 No. 160) (as amended).

6

STOPPING TREATMENT

Patient choice does not mean doing what the doctors want. Choice implies alternatives and we as patients are free to accept or reject medical treatment and advice. The whole idea of consent implies the possibility that we may give or withhold consent. In this chapter, we shall explore the circumstances, reasons and moral issues raised when patients and doctors decide to stop or to refuse treatment. Doctors are not in the business of preserving life at all costs and by every means. Sometimes doctors have to make the medical and moral decisions to stop treatment. Sometimes they decide not to start a treatment. These decisions are too important to be left to doctors and patients as separate individuals. This is where the partnership model is so important. It helps prevent doctors from playing god and yet provides us as patients with the information and advice we need to make appropriate decisions about what happens to us. Whatever we as a patient decide to do, doctors are never to abandon us. We are entitled to medical support and care in all circumstances. When we as patients choose to stop having active treatment, then doctors retain the responsibility to provide comfort and care.

For us to have patient choice involves having difficult options. These options include not only alternative treatments, but a decision between having treatment or refusing it. To make such choices, we need information and the freedom from pressure to make our own choices. The freedom of the individual is a right of both patients and doctors. As patients we cannot normally be forced to have treatment against our will. Similarly, doctors cannot be forced to give treatment they regard as pointless, morally wrong and not in the best interests of the patient. Patients and doctors may disagree, and so too will doctors with each other. The idea of how to judge best interests needs careful exploration and practical guidance for those facing such decisions. Doctors are at the sharp end of such decision-making if a patient is unable or unwilling to judge for himself or herself. The doctor will need to consider whether continuing treatment will benefit the patient, or whether stopping treatment is a better option. Normally, we as patients can and will be involved in such decisions, but when we are unable to give consent, then the responsibility falls on the doctor. He or she will consult colleagues and our family and friends, but the buck stops with the doctor.

Rise of Technology

Decisions about treatment and non-treatment depend partly on the kinds of treatment involved. For patients and doctors to make such choices, they need to know what is available. As technology advances, the range of treatment options has increased. The extent and degree of what technology is able to provide is remarkable but also poses its own problems. When we patients read about the latest technological advances in medicine, we often ask our doctor if we can have that treatment. Some have argued that doctors also have the mentality that if it is there, it must be used. If we have the technology then we should use it. Issues of cost have cast doubt on this attitude. Issues of morality and good medical practice are just as important and relevant. Doctors must not give in to patient, societal or personal pressure to use technology unless there is a clear benefit to the individual patient and unless the burden and painfulness of such treatment is not too great.

Doctors are increasingly recognising that some patients fear technology. Many patients are afraid that they will be forced to keep on living and kept alive artificially on life-support machines, when they would rather be allowed to die. As patients we can want to have our cake and eat it in relation to technology. If I collapse and am taken into hospital with a coronary attack, I expect 'high-tech' medicine to try to save my life. I am delighted that we in the UK have access to good medical technology and want it to be used, especially when I need it for myself or for my family. In contrast, I would not want to spend my life on an intensive-care machine, where there was no genuine quality of life and no prospect of improvement or recovery. In such circumstances my attitude towards technology is much less positive and I would want doctors to consider very carefully whether to use technology if all it does is prolong my dying.

Doctors are thus confronted with difficult and contradictory attitudes towards technology. It is a powerful and positive tool and works well when it is seen as a servant creating treatment options. It can become a master which drives doctors and patients to extraordinary lengths to avoid or delay death. Just because we have technology does not mean that we must use it. There is no technological imperative. Doctors need to make appropriate clinical decisions about the proper use of technology. We patients need to be free to refuse technological treatment, if that is our choice. Technology must not remove the autonomy of the patient or the professional judgement of the doctor.

The Law

In passing legal judgement on decisions to stop treatment or to continue treatment when a patient or family refuse consent, the presumption of the courts has generally been in favour of preserving human life. The courts recognise that the price of that prevention may be too high in terms of becoming an intolerable burden or being excessively painful for a patient. In these circumstances, treatment may be stopped or withdrawn in the best interests of the patient.

In February of 1993, the House of Lords made a key ruling on the withdrawal of treatment. Tony Bland was gravely injured in the Hillsborough football disaster. He was in a persistent vegetative state. He could not see, hear, taste, smell, speak or communicate in any way. He had no awareness. All those concerned agreed with the diagnosis and that the prognosis was that there was no hope of improvement or recovery. Because he was unable to give or withhold consent his doctors and family asked the courts' permission to discontinue all life-sustaining treatment and the medical measures designed to keep him alive. The key question was whether or not the doctors could withdraw ventilation, nutrition and hydration by artificial means. In other words, are doctors free to stop feeding patients in this state?

The House of Lords ruling stated that doctors are free to discontinue feeding and treatment in this case. The Law Lords took great pains to stress that each patient must be considered individually by the courts. This is to protect patients and doctors as well as to reassure families and the public. The Lords stressed that this was no charter to allow euthanasia but to suggest that society needs to debate what laws we should have in this area of medical technology and the withdrawal of treatment, food and water. They recognised that many people will be opposed to regarding the giving of food, even using a tube, as a medical treatment. These folk would argue that food and comfort are basic things all of us should have and things which doctors and nurses should never withdraw. The debate will continue and rage furiously, especially over what counts as the best interests of people in this state, what quality of life is involved, how limited resources should be used, and the roles of doctors, families and the courts in such decisions.[1]

The Moral Dimension
Choosing to stop treatment or not to be treated is not just a medical and personal decision, it is also a matter of morality.

(i)Patient autonomy
The trend towards increasing the choice and autonomy of the patient means that the views of the patient are the crucial factors in decisions to stop or continue treatment. Autonomy rests on being competent. People are only free to make their own decisions if they are able to make decisions properly. Society, through the law, makes provisions for those like children, the mentally disturbed and unconscious people, who are unable to make proper decisions for themselves. Most of us are considered competent, and that broadly means that our choices will be what most reasonable people would choose in the particular circumstances. If we are competent, we are free and able to choose not to have a treatment or to stop having a treatment, if there is a good reason for that choice. The ability to offer reasons is at the heart of what it means to be competent. A good reason does not have to be what the doctor likes or agrees with. If it is important to us, then we are able to express that decision and have

it respected. Doctors can only act against that decision if they are convinced that we are not really competent to make a decision at all and, in exceptional cases, where the law courts favour medical intervention in the best interests of the patient.[2]

(ii) Best interests

We patients are assumed to act in our own best interests. Where particular patients need protection from others or even from themselves, doctors justify such action on the basis that they are acting in the best interests of the patient. Doctors may have to justify that decision in the courts. The duties of a doctor are not to harm patients and to try to do what is good for them. Usually, these moral responsibilities are called non-maleficence and beneficence. Sometimes patients may not regard what doctors do as 'good for them'. To have your wishes disregarded and to be forced to carry on treatment would be a clear harm. To be required to endure pain from a new treatment, which you did not want, is not an obvious benefit to a patient. As patients we may decide it is in our best interests to be allowed to die. In the next chapter, we carefully distinguish this kind of request from the demand to be killed. Patients are properly free to ask and expect doctors to end their lives. We are in the best position to make judgements about what harms and benefits us and what is in our own best interests. Doctors are there to advise about the medical consequences of treatment and non-treatment decisions. They must also respect our wishes, if these are based on our own understanding of our interests.

In situations of terminal illness, individual patients may decide that they would prefer to be totally alert, even if it means a high level of pain. Some patients do not want pain-killers, even if they need them and would benefit from them. Most patients, however, do want and are entitled to expect pain-relief treatment. It is clearly in our best interests to be given what we want and need. We are in the best position to judge how much pain relief is required.[3] We need to understand that one effect of some pain-control medications will be to shorten life. The morality of such treatment is discussed in the Chapter on Suicide and Euthanasia. Here the stress is on our freedom of choice as patients and our own assessment of what is in our best interests. We are equally free to refuse pain relief and any treatment which we do not want. Cancer patients often decide that they do not want radiotherapy or chemotherapy. The prospect of prolonged treatment, or possible unpleasant side-effects, and all for a little more extended length or improved quality of life, make some patients opt for non-treatment. They are entitled to comfort, care and proper pain relief. Their decision not to be treated must be respected.

(iii) Acts and omission

We patients have the right to refuse treatment or to ask for it to be withdrawn. Doctors, too, may make a clinical decision not to begin a treatment, to withdraw some treatment, or to stop treating. Morally this is regarded by doctors as quite different from taking a positive step to kill someone. If treatment is stopped or not begun then death may occur. To many it will seem that there is little difference between doing something which will end life and stopping something, which means that death happens. That little difference is very important indeed. If a doctor or a patient decides to stop a treatment when the patient is suffering from a terminal illness then the patient will usually die. Death is likely, but not absolutely inevitable and certainly not at that particular moment when the treatment is stopped. If and when death does occur, it happens because of a terminal illness not because of the non-treatment decision. In the same way, if a doctor decides not to begin a treatment like resuscitation, then the patient will die because the patient is already dying. Nature is taking its course. It is disease that kills and not the doctor. There is no exact moment of death caused by non-treatment or omission of treatment, and there is no sensible way that such an omission can be considered the cause of death. Doctors are still responsible for omissions and non-treatment. This responsibility must be shared with the patient concerned if at all possible. The doctor will know that as a result of that decision, nature will take its inevitable course and the disease will end life. The death can be foreseen, but it is not the intention. Some doctors would say that when they decide not to continue or begin treatment, they make that choice intending that the patient die. That is more than likely true, but the fact of the matter is that they do not kill the patient. The disease kills. Good medicine allows doctors both to

stop and not to initiate treatment. We patients are free to refuse to be treated, and to ask for treatment to be withdrawn. In
neither case is this considered killing. The deliberate taking of life
is illegal, regarded by most people as immoral, and if permitted
would fundamentally affect the partnership between doctors and
patients (see pages 161 to 162 in the Chapter on Suicide and
Euthanasia).

(iv) Professional and personal

The British Medical Association and the General Medical Council, which together set and maintain the professional standards of
doctors, are adamant in their opposition to the deliberate taking
of life, but supportive of doctors and of patients who decide to
stop treatment. The particular problems of withdrawal of treatment
and what constitutes treatment are dealt with on pages 158 to
159 in the Chapter on Suicide and Euthanasia. The importance
of the GMC is that it provides a public scrutiny of such decisions where there is any suspicion of untoward conduct. The
law of the land makes its decisions about the legal justification
for withdrawing treatment. In addition, the professional bodies
issue advice to doctors. That advice has been consistently that
doctors are free to discontinue treatment and to decide not to
begin treatment, if they are convinced it is in the best interests
of the patient. Both the GMC and the BMA are equally clear
that patients should be totally involved in making such decisions
with the doctor and that the autonomy and choice of the patients
should be given the maximum respect. In cases of conflict, when a
compromise or agreement cannot be reached, the professional advice
to doctors is to obtain a legal ruling. Then the responsibility is
removed from the doctor and the patient. The court then takes that
responsibility and makes the decision.

Even when such legal decisions are made, doctors and patients will
have their own personal moral beliefs and attitudes. These beliefs will
affect their attitudes towards decisions about stopping treatment. For
some Roman Catholics and Jews, the refusal of life-saving treatment
is considered to be wrong. It is tantamount to suicide. The morality
of suicide in relation to medicine is discussed on pages 155 to 156
in the Chapter on Suicide and Euthanasia. The stress here is on the

fact that doctors and patients may have strong views about the sanctity of human life. This may mean that they think that life should be preserved at all costs. The quality of life may not be high, but that may be considered irrelevant as long as life is present. If a doctor has this view, it is important for patients to know about it and to recognise that it will fundamentally affect that doctor's attitude towards stopping treatment. He or she will not do it. Likewise, if we as patients have strong beliefs in the sanctity of life, the doctor needs to know that, for it will affect the options given to us and the likely decisions about non-treatment or treatment withdrawal. If there is conscientious objection to stopping treatment, then neither doctors nor patients can impose their views on each other. Doctors cannot force patients to carry on treatment and living. As patients we cannot force doctors to stop preserving our lives, if such a step would be against their consciences. In the end, we as patients have the final say if what we wish is within the law. Where a doctor cannot morally accept a patient's decision, then that patient should be transferred to another doctor who is willing.

Decisions to Stop Treatment or Not to Begin

Before considering the elements in the decision not to begin or to stop treatments, it must be clear that doctors can never stop providing comfort and care for their patients. The general grounds for a decision not to continue in treatment or not to begin treatment are: the wishes of the patient; the burden on the patient; the pointlessness of poor results; or economic resources. We patients may refuse treatment or ask that it be discontinued. This would usually be on the grounds that we do not regard it as in our best interests to have such treatments. That is the same standard used by doctors if patients are unable to make their own decision. Issues of quality of life and how we judge it are relevant to judgements about best interests. If there is no genuine prospect of recovery or benefit in giving a treatment, then it is pointless to continue to provide it. Increasingly, resource issues in terms of time and money will affect treatment decisions. The issues and impact on

our choices as patients are considered further on pages 206 to
221.

Withdrawing Treatment

It is much easier for all concerned if a decision is made not to begin
a treatment rather than having to withdraw it. The 'I've started so
I'll finish' attitude rests on the need to have a very good reason
to change a decision. Once the full force of medical treatment has
been used in life support then it is extremely painful to reverse that
decision. It can feel like a failure. It can appear to be inconsistent.
It seems to call into question the original decision. With such
pressures, doctors do prefer not to start rather than to be forced to
withdraw. The BMA does not believe that there is a moral difference
between withholding and withdrawing treatment. An opposite view
is argued for in dealing with euthanasia, as discussed in the BMA's
1988 'Euthanasia' report. Doctors are required to justify any decision
to stop or withdraw a treatment.

In a neonatal unit where severely handicapped babies are placed
in incubators at birth, their lives are being preserved. It takes time
to learn how severe the handicap will be and what kind of brain
damage has taken place. It also takes time for the parents to
begin to understand what has happened and what it will mean
for the baby to survive, both for the baby and for them. There
may come a time when the parents and the doctors and other staff
decide to stop treating the baby. The baby is then removed from
the incubator and allowed to die.

This scenario encapsulates well what is involved in a decision
to withdraw treatment. When needed and wanted, treatment is
supplied. If there is no longer any benefit to be gained from that
treatment, and it is futile to continue, then that treatment may be
withdrawn. That would be supported on the grounds that there is
no real benefit for the patient; the quality of life is so poor that such
a life is not worth living; it is not in the patient's best interests for
treatment to continue, and the waste of resources which could be used
for the genuine benefit of others is unjustifiable. These have been the
kinds of factors at work in decisions to withdraw life support from
people who are in a persistent vegetative state.[4] That never means

care and comfort will be withdrawn. Doctors are always required to give basic comfort and care for patients, regardless of the decisions made either by patients or by doctors for patients.

Patients' Consent

In an earlier chapter, we explored the notion of consent and saw that there were two sides to consent and choice. We patients can consent to or refuse treatment. We can opt for or against treatment to begin or to be stopped. Before any decision can be taken, doctors and patients need to have full and frank discussions. These discussions should be over a period of time, where the issues and their implications need to be understood and assimilated. Where these decisions affect life and death, the quality of that decision needs to be of the highest. Doctors must beware of pressurising patients even inadvertently. The way we present options to people can influence their decisions.

One doctor described how he would paint a very negative picture of one possibility and when he saw the negative reaction, he would present the one he wanted in a positive light. Patients always chose the second one. This was not a genuine choice. Doctors can fall into the trap of manipulating patients and their choices. Genuine discussion means that options are open and decisions free. It also requires full and proper information. We patients need to know what it will mean to have a treatment or to refuse it. The consequences – especially in terms of our quality of life, our degree of dependency on others, the physical and mental limitations we will experience – all need to be presented in as gentle a way as possible. None of us likes taking bad news, especially if it affects us directly. The prospects of personal deterioration, loss of abilities and independence, and in their place growing dependence and handicap, are not easy to accept. The difference that treatment will make, its side-effects and its limitations must be clear. The benefits and the drawbacks, the cost of those benefits in terms of length or quality of life, and the possible consequences have to be understood. It is not just the giving of the information itself which is important. It is also how we feel about the information. We are in the best position to decide what quality of life is desired and how much pain and distress we can cope with. When all the factors have been considered by us, the decision may be not to opt for treatment, even if it does provide some prospect of longer life.

Some doctors have felt that even giving patients this kind of detailed information was too difficult for patients to discuss. It might also be difficult for doctors to discuss it with patients. Even if we will be upset by such knowledge, most of us want to know what is going to happen to us. Doctors must be sensitive to the clues patients give about how much information we desire and when we want to have it. As patients we will need ongoing support from doctors as we work through and come to terms with what faces us and the choices that need to be made.

Patients' Refusal

The general principle in medicine and law is that treatment cannot be given or continued against the wishes of a patient who is competent and able to decide for herself or himself. It may be very difficult for medical and nursing staff to cope with a patient's decision to refuse treatment. This is all the more difficult if the staff would not have decided the same thing; have advised the patient to do the opposite; and the known result of the decision will be a death, which could have been avoided or delayed. This is the price doctors pay for respecting patient autonomy. It is not the doctor's fault and responsibility that patients may choose badly. It is only the doctor's fault if they have not given proper information and not enabled the patient to understand the benefits of treatment and the results of a refusal. When a patient refuses treatment, if the medical staff disagree with that decision, they should explore why it has been refused. If there are misapprehensions and misunderstandings, these should be corrected. If there are alternatives, these should be offered. At no time must the patient feel that comfort and care will be removed if an unpopular decision is reached.

In emergencies, doctors have to assume that patients would want to be treated. This is what happens in cases of attempted suicide. Doctors try to save the person's life. It may have been a serious and carefully considered decision of this person to take their own life. If the patient arrives in hospital, doctors are entitled to assume that treatment should be given. The patient's own mental state may have been disturbed. If there is any reasonable doubt about the patient's competence, then the doctor must act to save life. It is quite wrong to assume that because a person has chosen to die, that he or she is incompetent. People have good reasons to end their lives. An emergency situation is not the place to assess the rationality of a suicide attempt. If life-saving means are needed, the doctor must treat, even if afterwards the patient is unhappy and makes it clear that the suicide attempt was genuine and will be repeated.

We patients have the right to refuse treatment and do. Jehovah's Witnesses are a clear example where religious beliefs affect attitudes towards blood products and treatments like transfusions which involve such blood products. Doctors must respect the wishes of all patients with such views. If they are unwilling to continue as a doctor in relation to such patients, they should refer them to another doctor. If there is genuine doubt about the competence of a patient or the need to protect children in such circumstances, the courts should be consulted.[5]

Competent to refuse?

For those who are not competent either to accept or refuse treatment, doctors, carers, families and friends take responsibility. Usually the aim behind such decision-making is to allow treatment to take place. It might also include decisions to stop treatment. One possible standard to be used is some indication of what the patient might have wanted. This is hard to know and even harder to check. We might never have considered what might happen and what our response might be. Some patients might not be able to take such an imaginative step. Even if they could and did, the doctor is unlikely to have access to independent corroboration. The doctor might then resort to what other reasonable people would choose in the same circumstances. While this does point to consistency, it assumes uniformity. People do vary tremendously and what we want and decide about our own lives may be very different. Trying to assess an acceptable quality of life for someone else is also fraught with difficulty. None of us would want to live the life of a severely handicapped person. But that judgement is made from the perspective of the fit and able-bodied. If a handicapped life was the only life we had and knew, our perspective on its worth and value might be very different. Great care should be taken in assessing other people's quality of life. We are not justified in stopping treatment just because we would not want to live like that. The best interests of the patient must be considered. That holds true when we patients are not able or competent to express what we want.

Advance Directives or Living Wills

There is an increasing move towards patients expressing their wishes in the event of some accident or progressive disease, in the form of an advance directive. This states what we would like done and what we do not want done. It provides a written and witnessed proof of what we wanted at the time of signing it. As such, it gives doctors one indication of what patients thought they wanted. Such advance directives must be discussed with and witnessed by a doctor. They provide an excellent opportunity for doctors and patients to discuss the unthinkable and what should be done if it were to happen. The particular form many such directives take is to indicate that we would not wish to be treated aggressively, or to become dependent on a life-support system, or to have drugs which would only prolong dying, and would wish to be treated with dignity and respect. This is very different from asking doctors to kill. That is discussed further in the Chapter on Suicide and Euthanasia.

While living wills may be a useful indication of the patient's attitude, they do not provide an absolute assurance. They may have been drawn up many years before. Doctors will not feel that they or their patients are necessarily to be bound by something signed at eighteen if the patient is now eighty. Our attitude to life and its value may change as the years go by. Doctors are also concerned that new medical advances and treatments may have been unknown to the patient. Rapid changes may fundamentally alter the treatment of disease and the quality of life of patients. Advance directives give useful indications of the patient's wishes, but do not provide cast-iron guarantees that they did not change their minds.

There may be practical problems of locating the directive. It might only come to light after a treatment has begun. The directive might indicate that this was not what the patient wanted.

Doctors must follow the wishes of the patient, unless there are overriding clinical indications to the contrary, or doubt over the rationality of such wishes. Advance directives are not only relevant when patients are terminally ill. If patients are concerned about what might happen if they were severely handicapped or brain-damaged and left in a quadraplegic or persistent vegetative state, such directives would provide a clear account of the wishes of the patient and should be respected.

In some countries, a proxy may be appointed to make decisions for patients in certain circumstances, when and if the patient is unable to make a decision. The proxy offers a judgement, acting as a substitute for the patient. The proxy will know the patient well and be aware of his or her values, beliefs and attitudes to life, its prolongation and the stopping of treatment. A proxy has no status in law except in a very limited way in Scotland. Patients may appoint a proxy and complete a living will. The proxy can then interpret what the patient would want in circumstances which may not have been envisaged by the patient in the dreaming up of the directive.

The Basis for Refusing Treatment for Others

(i) Best interests

Doctors have a dual responsibility to and for us as patients. They are to preserve life and alleviate suffering. Sometimes these two different aims conflict. Pain-relieving drugs may shorten life. We patients may also have to choose between living longer or having a better quality of life for a shorter time. The price paid for survival may be regarded as too high for us in terms of pain and discomfort. In the name of best interests we may opt to forgo treatment. Our choice as a patient is the crucial factor.

If we are unable to make a choice, then carers, families and doctors will have to consider what is in our best interests and act accordingly. As a rough guide in deciding whether or not a treatment which prolongs life is really in the best interests of a patient, the doctor and others must understand the patient's beliefs and values and must look at the patient's life, its quality and its limits.

Doctors will need to know how the patient is likely to react to their situation if life is prolonged or if treatment is not given. The balance between the mere extension of life and what has to be done to the patient for this to happen, needs to be finally judged. In a medical setting, the presupposition on the part of doctors tends to be in favour of treatment. It should rather rest on our best interests as patients. What most people would regard as a reasonable quality of life or too high a price to be paid, will offer some indication of what a doctor should do.

(ii) Quality of life

We have clearly indicated that no one can easily make quality-of-life decisions about other people's lives. Medical science is not able to be absolutely certain what quality of life will follow every treatment or no treatment at all. Life itself is precious and to be preserved. If life is affected by handicap or disability, it remains life and there must be overwhelming grounds presented for destroying that life. For most people, it is not life itself which is the all important thing. The quality of that life is what matters. Life has to be worth living for most of us. Sanctity accepts that some lives may be allowed to come to an end. In the Abortion Law, killing is justified. There is clearly no absolute value placed on life itself in our pluralistic society. In a world of scarce resources, where patient choice and autonomy is central, it is not surprising that more and more attention is being given to how to assess the quality of life.

In situations where the life in question is severely limited and there is little or no ability to relate to others or to experience what most people regard as normal things, then some will doubt that the quality of such a life is worth living. Others will argue that such a life may not be what most of us want, but that in no way can justify ending that life. In the case of a baby born with severe brain damage, the courts decided that nature could be allowed to take its course if life were regarded as intolerable and an extreme burden.[6] While rejecting any idea that positive steps may be taken to kill such a person, the court recognised that doctors cannot and ought not to be required to preserve all life at all costs, if that life is so poor that most people in the same circumstances would want it ended. Both to refuse treatment or to treat is permitted for patients and doctors. As we have stressed already, care and comfort must always be provided regardless of the quality of the life being cared for.

The Duties of Doctors

Medical skill, expertise and experience enable a doctor to predict how a decision will develop and what would happen to a patient if different treatments were given. Knowing the patient and what he or she might want, families and doctors can discuss the alternatives. If there is no clear indication of what the patient would wish to happen, then the decision to treat or stop treatment depends on the assessment of the patient's best interests by others. It is not always possible to reach unanimous agreement about what those best interests are. A mother might feel that a child with terminal leukaemia or cancer has suffered enough from the disease and the treatment of that disease. She might refuse more treatment for her child. Doctors might feel that there were still good grounds for more treatment, in the hope of further delaying the disease and leaving room for the possibility of remission. The disagreement would focus on how much difference the treatment would actually make, the risk of further harm, and the lack of certainty over the length of survival time. When doctors and parents disagree, then the final recourse is to law. Doctors are not always right and need to beware of putting pressure on families to agree with the medical decision, even against their own better judgement. Consultation may lead to an agreed solution. Doctors should be guided by the inside information from relatives and friends, but that might not override clinical judgements. The doctor must always have the patient's best interests at heart.

In team settings, doctors have the advantage of other professional perspectives and advice. In the case of a life-and-death decision, we as patients can be assured that no decision will be made by doctors without the widest consultation possible and careful scrutiny and review before any action is taken. Controversial decisions should be the particular object of careful scrutiny.

Do Not Resuscitate

For the avid media watchers, resuscitation has invaded homes and is no longer done behind closed doors. For many years, doctors have been operating a rough and ready process of deciding who should live and who should be allowed to die. This took the form of a directive written in the notes or, even worse, at the bedside, not to resuscitate. Even if this did occur, the atmosphere and attitude to such decisions have changed. They are no longer made secretly, without consultation, but openly, after frank discussions with patients, families and other professional colleagues. If a patient has a heart attack, or breathing stops, then resuscitation could take place. The dying process involves the stopping of the heart and breathing. Everyone could be given resuscitation, even if it is not always possible to regain life. Decisions must be made about when it is appropriate to resuscitate and when it would be wrong. The consultant is ultimately responsible for the decision and for making sure all the relevant staff know what has been decided and the basis for it. Problems have arisen when different shifts of doctors have not been party to the decisions. Good communication is vital.

That still leaves the hard question of who should be resuscitated. The BMA and the Royal Colleges of Nursing and Anaesthetists have produced agreed guidelines. These provide a basic framework to help local settings make their own decisions about resuscitation. The key elements are a stress on the ultimate responsibility of the consultant for the decision and the progress of consultation. That consultation should involve the patient, the rest of the care team, relatives and friends. If the patient has a clear view and does not wish to be resuscitated, that should be recorded in the patient's notes and respected. The general rule is not to resuscitate when the patient has made his or her refusal clear over a sustained period of time, or where the quality of life restored would be unacceptable to the patient, or when such resuscitation is futile and unlikely to be successful.[7]

It is quite clear, in conclusion, that our choice as patients must cover both the consent to treatment and its refusal. We are free to reject treatment options as long as we are competent. Even if the reasons for such refusal may seem bizarre, doctors have no right to countermand such a decision unless there is genuine doubt as to our competence. Where we are unable to make such a serious decision then the doctor must consult as widely as possible. Advance directives might offer an indication of a particular patient's wishes at an earlier stage. While helpful, they cannot be binding on a doctor. Where a patient is incompetent, the doctor and families must consider the quality of life, best interests and known views of the patient towards stopping treatment. Our choice as patients remains the underpinning of treatment and non-treatment decisions.

Questions about Stopping Treatment

Do I want to discontinue treatment?

Do I understand what will happen if I stop treatment or refuse to be treated?

Has my doctor explained the effects and consequences of my decision to stop or refuse treatment?

Have I discussed my decision with my family and friends?

Am I convinced that I will be given all the pain relief, care and comfort I need?

If not, have I made my worry and fear on this score plain to the doctors and nurses?

If my death is likely to follow from my decision to stop a treatment, what is my doctor's attitude to the sanctity of life?

Do I have strong views about the sanctity of life and do I understand the implications of my belief for my treatment?

Am I prepared to continue with this quality of life or do I want to stop treatment?

Have I discussed and made it clear with my family what I want to happen in the event of an accident or if I need resuscitation, life-support or extraordinary treatment?

Have I drawn up a living will or advance directive?

Have I discussed this with my doctor and family?

Am I clear about what I want to happen if the living will becomes necessary?

Have I kept it up to date?

Have I changed my mind since I signed it?

Is it readily available if it is needed?

Notes to Chapter 6
1. *Airedale NHS Trust* v. *Bland*, House of Lords (4 February 1993).
2. *See* 'Rights and Responsibilities of Doctors', *British Medical Journal* (1992), 1ff.
3. The National Council for Hospice and Palliative Care Services has vast information on this theme.
4. *Airedale NHS Trust*, *op. cit.*
5. NHS Circular HSC (GEN) 81 (1975).
6. Re J (A Minor) (Wardship: medical treatment) (1990) 3 AER 930 CA.
7. Letter from the Chief Medical Officer (PL/CMO (91)22); *see also* the agreed guidelines from the BMA and Royal Colleges of Nurses and Anaesthetists.

7

CARE OF THE DYING

Death is one certainty that faces us all. Woody Allen expressed the attitude of most of us when he said: 'I'm not afraid of dying. I just don't want to be there when it happens.' Doctors are trained to preserve life. It is very hard for them to come to terms with death and dying. Death itself can often be seen as some kind of defeat. Sometimes medicine seems determined to resist death at all costs. Yet death is inevitable and doctors have a duty and a responsibility to help us as patients as we face the last hurdle.

It is hard for us to imagine being dead. Death is not just the end of our life. It feels like the final stopping of everything. Religious folk believe that there is life after death, but even personal faith does not always seem to help people face death easily. Our own death is quite different from that of other people. When someone else dies that is just another event in the rest of our lives. Our own death is the end of all experience and events as we know them. There is a finality about death, and a fear for many of nothingness or of not knowing what is beyond the grave.

Part of the fear of death in our society seems to relate to the absence of direct experience of death. There is much less child death, and most of us live longer. It is quite normal for people not to have a bereavement before they are in mid-life. Few of us have seen a dead body. Death mostly takes place in hospital. Bodies are kept in Chapels of Rest rather than at home. The cultural trappings of death are few and far between. When my father died in my childhood, the closing of the coffin, 'the chesting', was an event. Even at the funeral people came to the house expecting to view the body. Society's attitude to death has changed and this affects our own attitude to dying and to those who are dying. Living is normal. Dying is abnormal, so the terminally ill may be all too easily marginalised. If it is mostly elderly folk who die, then they are often alone, with no family near at hand. We are not very good as a society in coming to terms with the reality of death and dying. We do not know what to say or how to say it. The advent of HIV and AIDS has begun to affect our perception of death. Fit and healthy young people are contracting a fatal disease and dying. Care for them and their own example has challenged traditional attitudes towards death and may, in an ironic way, help society face up to and so cope better with involvement with people who are dying.

The Role of the Doctor

As technology has pushed back the frontiers of death, doctors have been increasingly faced with the reality of life and death decisions. Where there was little that could be done, people just died. Now a great deal can often be done to delay death. That may not just preserve life. It may also prolong the process of dying. In general practice, the doctor gets to know his or her patients very well. The doctor is a visitor to patients' homes and sees us sometimes in health and sometimes in illness from the cradle to the grave. Given the partnership relation between doctors and patients, the help and support of the GP will be vital for the dying patient. Ideally, death will have been discussed by the two. One of the advantages for patients of a move to have advance directives or living wills will be that the patient will have to discuss what he or she wants with the doctor. Knowing the patient will enable the doctor to assess what the patient wants, how much information will be appropriate and when that information should be given. The doctor will also know the patient's views about treatment, when it is appropriate, how far such treatment should go, and in what circumstances the patient would wish to be allowed to die and what arrangements should be made after death.

Death affects not just the dead, but also the living. The pain of death continues in the distress of bereavement. Families, friends and carers may be deeply affected by the death of a loved one. The doctor will be required to support them over a period of time, which may be longer rather than shorter. It is remarkable how much illness occurs during the first year of a bereavement. As others are affected by a person's death at the moment of dying, so they too have an input on the dying person. Relatives may create problems for those who are terminally ill. Patients may not wish their families to know that they are dying. Patients may be under pressure to go into hospital or a home, when they would much rather remain at home. Relatives may force a patient to opt for or against treatment because of financial or other factors, which may have little or nothing to do with the patient's best interests. Doctors have a responsibility to ensure that patients are not under pressure from families and relatives to make decisions, which may not be genuine choices and may even be harmful.

Privacy and the dying patient

Doctors have duties of confidentiality to patients. The privacy of personal information may feel even more important to a dying patient. The doctor must preserve that confidentiality, unless there is some very serious risk to others. In such settings, the doctor should encourage the patient to consent to the doctor sharing the information. This might arise for those who are dying from AIDS. Consent and confidentiality are but two aspects of the doctor–patient partnership which flourish and are preserved where there is good communication. Doctors are increasingly being trained in the art of good communication. In situations of terminal care and of death, doctors need to come to terms with their own mortality. Those who work in neonatal units and have to cope with the death of premature babies and the natural parental grief, report that they themselves all too easily become emotionally involved. If they have their own children, the distress is all the greater.

In training doctors, good models are important. Dissecting a dead body in an anatomy class is very different from being present when someone you know dies. In the recent past, death seemed more like the ultimate failure of medicine and an enemy to be resisted at all costs. Attitudes are changing, though, because as patients some of us are afraid of meddlesome medicine, and do not want doctors to prolong the process of death. We may not want lots of medical technology forced on us for little gain of time and a great deal of pain and distress. As patients we want to have our choices and our own person respected. We want to be allowed to die with dignity. We want comfort and tender loving care, and the assurance that we will not be left to face death alone, unless that is our wish.

Doctors have a key role in the care of the dying, and their own understanding of patients, death, the dying process and how they should respond to it has been fundamentally affected by the development of the hospice movement.

The Hospice Movement

Public perception of the work of hospices tends to focus on the care they provide for the terminally ill. In fact, the hospice movement has made a further major initiation to modern medicine by pioneering work in pain control and relief. The total care of the individual who is terminally ill is provided by the hospices. This has often been funded by local committees and by the efforts of enthusiastic volunteers. It is only gradually that local health authorities have accepted some degree of financial responsibility for hospice care. That care is not just on a residential basis in hospices. It involves a wide range of home care services ranging from round-the-clock support to counselling. The keynote of hospice care is the whole person. Physically, emotionally, mentally, socially and spiritually, people need to be cared for and supported. This care is provided in a setting of openness and honesty. Doctors and other staff seek to communicate clearly and sympathetically with the patient, recognising the different stages we pass through as we try to come to terms with the fact and experience of our own dying. Hospices also encourage patients to communicate with their families. Patients are not seen or treated as isolated units and are respected in their family and community settings. A level of personal and psychological support is matched by control of symptoms and pain relief. It seems that most of us are more afraid of the pain involved in death than in death itself. The hospice movement promises and delivers pain relief for most of the people most of the time. There is no one hundred per cent pain relief available, and some doubt whether there ever will be, or even whether it would be a good idea to create an environment totally free of pain. The reality is that pain relief is increasingly available for patients, not just in hospices, but wherever the lessons of pain control have been learned. It is important that doctors involved in other areas of medicine do discover the lessons of pain relief and begin to practise control of pain as a regular part of their care of patients.

The Cox case

In a court case a Doctor Cox was charged with attempted murder of one of his patients. His justification was that the patient was in extreme agony and that the only way to help her was to give her a fatal injection. Both the courts and the General Medical Council disagreed. This was attempted murder and Doctor Cox was found guilty. Medical experts confirmed to the GMC that pain-relief methods were available to help, but had not been properly used. This was corroborated by the decision of Doctor Cox's home hospital base to require him to attend a course on pain relief before returning to work.[1]

The hospice movement has produced a vast range of literature, video material and stimulated public debate and interest on every aspect of death, care of the dying and the bereavement process. Not all patients wish to take advantage of hospice care. There remains on the part of some a sense of unease and even a stigma about going into a hospice. Many patients who do enter a hospice return home and are able to live well and comfortably. Hospices are not just places to die. They are also places where people gain important respite care, recover and go home.

The spiritual dimension of life has been at the centre of the hospice movement from the very start. Many patients and staff have spiritual beliefs and needs. In facing death, people are confronted with fundamental spiritual issues. In a multi-faith society, all medical institutions must recognise how important such spiritual perspectives are to many of us patients. Doctors must be sensitive to the spiritual dimensions of patient care. This is part of what total care for the whole person involves. We as patients are not just bodies. We have minds and many believe that we have a spirit or soul, which is the essential person. The good doctor tries to deal with all of these aspects and elements of human beings in providing care for the dying.

The Problems of Controlling Pain

Doctors are people too, and working with patients who are dying will raise many personal issues about life and death, as well as beliefs and values. Such personal questions must not disrupt the responsibility for and care of the patient. Treating patients who are dying can pose some particularly hard problems for the doctors involved. While many of these problems are not in principle different from those in all patient care, what is different is their intensity and pressure.

The doctor's first responsibility is to control the patient's pain. Until and unless the patient is comfortable, there can be no proper communication and no real treatment planning, consultation and patient choice. Diseases have symptoms. Pain can result both from the disease itself or from the symptoms and effect of the disease. People with cancer may have pain from the cancer, but they may also be constipated, lack appetite, not be sleeping well, and generally be anxious and worrying about what will happen. These physical and psychological symptoms must be treated and controlled, as well as the specific pain for the cancer. When a patient is confident that the doctor can and will help control pain, then the partnership and good communication can develop.

In the past, pain control was much less refined. Too large doses of drugs often reduced the patient to a zombie-like existence. Nowadays, pain control emphasises the relief of pain while maintaining a patient's awareness and control of themselves. Patient need and demand are the basis for pain relief. Every patient is not simply given the same standard doses. Individual pain relief is given because each person is a different individual. We have different experiences of pain and different pain thresholds. We vary over how much pain we want to have and how much relief we will accept. There is an art to pain relief as well as a science. In the partnership, the doctor provides individualised pain control. We as patients choose the extent of pain relief.

Building Relationships

Doctors often describe it as a great privilege to share in the most intimate and personal experiences of patients. Caring for someone in the transition from life to death, especially if that is a slow and possibly painful process, is not easy. Deep emotions are aroused and the limits of what medicine can and ought to do have to be coped with. Medical training used to emphasise the need for objectivity. For doctors to attain this standard, they were encouraged not to become too involved with their patients. A healthy distance meant better treatment. It was a kind of protection for doctors, who could shield themselves from their own feelings by being detached and not getting involved. It is impossible to be nothing but objective about the process of dying. When patients face physical and mental deterioration, doctors need to understand what that means for a patient. They must ask themselves how they would feel in such circumstances.

Doctors expressing their feelings

If doctors were only involved in the technical care of the dying, when medical techniques failed then there would be nothing more for a doctor to do. As patients we do not want doctors to see us as interesting cases, but as people. We need a quality of relationship with a doctor. That is a very great demand. It is a deeply satisfying experience for doctors, as well as a privilege. In such a relationship, doctors have become vulnerable and are willing and able to express their emotions and reactions in discussion with patients.

Doctors are increasingly seeing that sharing their weaknesses and feelings with patients strengthens the partnership and feeling of mutuality. A stress on the choices of patients, autonomy, confidentiality and consent does not undermine the close partnership between a doctor and a patient. Nor is this relationship weakened by expecting doctors to use all of their medical skills, expertise and scientific training in treatment and care. The personal relationship between a doctor and patient is as important as the professional one. When conducted properly, both enhance, enable and enrich the other. Trust and confidence are important in this relationship of being partners. For this to be fostered and grow, doctors need to see that we patients are people with a network of concerns and relationships. The doctor will want to know our values and attitudes regarding life and death, pain and suffering, and medical treatment and its limits. What is best for any particular patient, but especially for one who is dying, is care which is appropriate to that individual person. The variety of a patient's needs must be responded to and doctors have recognised their own limits here. They have increasingly operated as part of a hospice team, where there are many skills, and professional groups work closely together to ensure the care of the whole patient in a holistic way. That doctors should have good relationships with each other and with patients is vital. A doctor needs the qualities of loving care, sympathy and empathy, and good levels of communication. A genuine commitment to the well-being of the patient and personal warmth will build the best doctor–patient partnership.

Acting with compassion

When we as patients move from life into death, our disease will increasingly affect us, but so too will our attitude and psychological state change, ebb and flow. Doctors will need to help us cope with and manage our death. We patients may not be in a state to communicate what is happening very clearly, but there may be obvious signals to doctors and other staff, often marked by our different behaviour. There may come a time when we are tired of the struggle to hold on to life and want to let go. It is inappropriate then for doctors to 'force' heroic treatments on us at such a stage. Rather, it may be time to stop treatment and to provide comfort and good levels of pain relief.

Most patients hate pretence. In the past, doctors often conspired with relatives to pretend that everything was all right and that the patient would get better. Sometimes even patients allowed and encouraged such collusion with doctors. While many patients still pass through a stage of the denial of death, they usually come to a more honest acceptance of reality. Once doctors pretend with patients, then the danger that doctors might always be pretending means that we cannot rely on knowing the truth and being helped to face the reality of death and dying. Families in particular can pressurise doctors to be upbeat and optimistic about recovery, even when the opposite is called for and death inevitable. Telling lies, misleading patients and not enabling all concerned to come to terms with reality are wrong for doctors. Patients and families need time and help to face up to death. That demands sensitivity yet strength from the doctor to resist any pressure to pretend. There must be no unrealistic or false hopes given to families or to patients. To do that is to hinder us from coping and working through our reactions to arrive at a point of acceptance. It must be said that some patients will never accept the reality of death. Families too can try to ignore and deny what is really happening. Doctors must not encourage such dishonesty, while still understanding what is happening and why. Helping people through such denial by gentle yet consistent presentation of the medical situation and giving support for their reactions is the duty of the doctor.

What the Patient Needs

It takes two to make a relationship and the other side of what the doctor must do is what we as patients need and expect. Pain control and relief have already been mentioned. We patients need to know that our pain can and will be controlled and that we will have as much awareness of what is going on around us as we wish for and medical science can provide. We patients must be in control of our own pain relief, drawing on the doctor's skill. We know best what we need and should be given appropriate drugs to ensure our comfort.

Good communication

The choices of patients do not simply focus on treatment and pain relief. To make such choices, we as patients need to know what is happening to us. We need to be fully informed. As patients we also need help in assimilating the information we have been given. We may be told that we are dying. We are often in the foreign environment of a hospital. We have little or no knowledge of the technicalities of medicine and are unfamiliar with the jargon of the medical world. Patients are often confused, distressed and fearful. Doctors must be sensitive to all these possibilities. As patients we need time and help to come to terms with information about our death. We may need to be told a number of times what is going on and what will happen. An individual patient may not want to know just at that moment, for there might be good reasons to put off knowing and having to tell others. A mother or father might delay learning all the facts until after a wedding, in order not to spoil the day for everyone, including him or herself. As patients we must be in control over how much information we wish to have and when we want to receive it.

We, as patients, expect to be able to discuss things with our doctor. In surveys the one thing most of us as patients seem to want from our doctors is more time. We want time to talk, to be listened to, and to understand what is happening. Doctors must work hard at ensuring good communication and we patients should never feel that we have not been heard properly. Part of the onus for such communication must rest on us as patients. If the doctor seems hesitant, then we should take the initiative.

The truth

We stressed that doctors should not tell lies or pretend with us. There is a subtle kind of pretence which suggests that medicine knows everything exactly. Doctors and medicine are limited. There are many things doctors do not know. We as patients need to be aware of the knowledge doctors do and do not have. This is especially important when doctors cannot be certain of how long a particular patient may take to die and where doctors do not know how to treat certain diseases. Doctors do not always know how far a disease has spread or how quickly a person's body or mind may deteriorate. Doctors are not omniscient. They must not pretend that they know everything. Patients likewise need to come to terms with such limits and recognise that as patients we cannot expect doctors to be able to do everything. Doctors are concerned to sustain a patient's hope and confidence. Where there is hope, then the possibility of recovery and the success rate of the treatment are often much better. It may be that some patients do not want to be told of the doctor's limits and uncertainties. Doctors need to be sensitive to this, not force more distress and unease on patients, but resist pretence and refuse to collude. Patients should be gently encouraged to face reality as it is without false hope. Otherwise, we may delay in dealing with personal and family matters which require sorting out before death.

The other side of the coin of refusing to pretend is to tell the truth. Honesty and frankness between doctor and patient is vital for a good partnership. There can be conflict between different principles in some cases. Doctors may feel that it is not in the best interests of a patient for them to be told the truth. This decision must be clearly based on the genuine best interests of the patient and not just for the benefit of the doctor who may find it difficult to broach the topic of dying. Doctors can be subjective, and can make flawed assumptions about what a patient does or does not want. The more communication and trust there is the more natural it will be to give painful information in an appropriate way with careful timing. The patient's choice is the key. If we do not want to know, then we must be free to make that choice. Most of us as patients will choose to know as much as possible about what is happening to us. Doctors should assume that patients want information, unless there are clear indications to the contrary.

Conflicts in Choices

Patient choice and autonomy do not necessarily clash with trust and confidence in the doctor. In fact, it is because of such trust and confidence that as patients we will be able to make our own choices and feel that our autonomy and our own selves are being properly respected. Some patients can abuse the relationship with a doctor. After a cycle of treatment, where there is no real medical indication for continuing that treatment, patients can demand more treatment. Patients may even demand to see another doctor in a refusal to come to terms with information and realities we do not want to accept. It may be easiest and best for a doctor in such a situation to provide another doctor and so another medical opinion. In the process of dying, it is not surprising that patients may criticise doctors for not doing enough. While there may be rare cases of neglect, the trend is to do all that a patient reasonably wants and expects. Patients cannot have it both ways. We cannot complain that doctors do not do enough, at the same time as criticising them for doing too much. As patients we can expect doctors to do their very best for us. Treatment or medical decisions should never be imposed on patients. Full discussion, information and communication should take place and mutual agreement be sought for and arrived at.

Doctors are responsible to the individual patient to avoid harm not just to him or her but to their other patients. That may be by making sure that resources are not wasted. If, in the doctor's clinical judgement, a treatment is a waste of time and money and/or will harm the patient, we cannot expect the doctor to provide such treatment. Indeed, the doctor has a duty to warn the patient of the risk of harm and to explain the reasons for refusing to provide that particular treatment. Even then, the patient must not be abandoned by the doctor. The patient can expect continuing care from the doctor. Patient demands are always to be seen in the light of wider needs and responsibilities. Dying patients can attempt to 'blackmail' doctors and relatives. Such inappropriate demands must be firmly resisted by doctors. Dying patients have no more or less rights, autonomy and choice than any other patient. The known shortening of time and life expectancy may give an emotional edge to dealing with such patients. It does not give extra rights. The excellent quality of care and pattern of relationships seen in hospice care should be what all doctors provide and all patients can expect.

Confidentiality and Respect

Patients may need to be protected from their relatives. Families can put pressure on a dying person to go into hospital, to have yet more treatment, or to stop having treatment. Patients have the right not to tell their families all they know. In the past, doctors often told relatives bad news and kept such information from the patient. This is a clear breach of trust and confidentiality. Patients have the right to know what is going on and, while most of us will want to discuss this with our family and should be encouraged to do so, each patient is free to ask the doctor to keep that information confidential. In medical care, doctors learn a great deal about the personal problems of people. Doctors may become involved in discussing all kinds of moral and spiritual issues with patients, who do not wish such conversations to be shared with families or friends. The right to privacy must be respected. One of the hardest things for any doctor is accepting when a patient does not wish medical or personal help although such help is needed and available. Allowing other people to make choices which will not help, and may even harm, is painful. Doctors will struggle when patients refuse help, but must respect the patient's rights and freedoms. Choice can be bad as well as good. If patient choice is itself the key, then bad choices must be accepted along with good ones.

A Good Death

Dying is something that happens to us. Doctors are not in the business of killing people, as we shall see in the next chapter. Patients can only expect that doctors will provide the very best care, treatment and pain relief that is available. As death approaches, those involved with the care of the patient will need to be sensitive and aware of the fears and needs of the patient. Doctors must alleviate pain, even if that also leads to a shortening of life (see the next chapter). As patients we need reassurance that we will have as easy a death as possible. Families and friends may want to be part of the final moments of life. Patients rarely want to die alone. Having someone to hold our hand as we move from this life is a basic human comfort. It may be important to sort out with our families and friends our relationships, finances, funeral wishes and what will happen after we die. Doctors must both encourage and support patients in these steps, realising that they will be extremely painful for all concerned. One sign that the doctor–patient relationship is working well is that as patients we feel free to discuss all these things with our doctor. It is part of the total care of the whole person, which is the mark of much of our care for the dying. We patients hope that this quality of care and partnership will be the norm in all of medicine rather than the exception.

Defining Death

Following a conference of the Medical Royal Colleges and their Faculties in the United Kingdom in January 1979, there was an agreed definition of death which is 'brainstem death'. In cases where death occurs unexpectedly the doctor might well make a report to the coroner. The coroner in turn may require a post-mortem, in accordance with the Coroners' Act 1988. Deaths must be registered and a doctor's signature and death certificate are required. Before a cremation can take place the doctor must sign a certificate, as required by the Births and Deaths Registration Act 1953. Even in death itself, doctors play a key role.

Problems for the Carers

When talking with hospice staff, one regular theme I raise with them is: 'Who cares for the carers?' There are many different levels to that care and who needs it. It usually begins with the family, partner and friends. Such care may be involved from the very start of treatment and care for the patient. The patient's death and dying process will inevitably affect other people. They will be called on to support the dying person. They too will have to face the reality of death and the awareness of loss that will follow. They will have to endure helplessly the pain of a loved one and often be unable to make any difference at all. Their own lives will be disrupted and their future will be uncertain. Doctors and other staff must be sensitive to the pressures on families in caring for their loved one. Hospices have created support groups for carers, which help prepare them for the death of the person cared for and to work through the various stages of that process from hearing the bad news to bereavement. Such support may continue for many years. It is a comfort to patients to know that their loved ones are being cared for and supported at a time when the patients may be least able to offer any support.

Handling feelings of guilt

After a patient's death, guilt may be a common feeling. That guilt might arise from a sense of regret that carers did not do more, could have done better, or that some problem areas of relationships were not really resolved. It may also be a sense of guilt arising from the fact that the carers are relieved that death has finally happened. It is difficult for us to admit that we may be glad that someone is dead. This is not because of some evil attitude, but the natural and almost inevitable reaction to a prolonged period of strain, disruption and pain. Carers may be glad for the person who has died and relieved for themselves. They may also feel guilty about those senses of relief. Hospice teams, GPs and any doctor who has contact with bereaved people must be aware of the possible impact of death and loss and give the necessary help and support.

Medical and nursing staff, social workers and all who are involved with dying patients will need help too. There is a high price to be paid for caring for the dying. The most professional people are still affected by death and they are better doctors and nurses because they are affected. Doctors who have lost the capacity to be affected by pain and death are less than human and unsympathetic doctors. Most staff will feel a sense of loss, even if they have only known the patient for a short time. The sheer intensity of caring for the dying makes very strong relationships. The constant exposure to the pain and suffering of others can lead to a sense of helplessness, hopelessness and frustration at medical and personal limitations. We all have to recognise that there are limits to what we can cope with. Being a doctor does not provide immunity from 'burnout'.

Doctors are increasingly encouraged to share their anger, frustration and reactions to death in support settings to help them gain perspective, to cope and to build even better relationships with those who are dying. Part of this is basic survival for those who work daily at the sharp end of death. It is not always an easy business, for it means admitting needs and limitations as well as finding time in a busy and demanding setting to make room for oneself. The work of continuing education, audit and appraisal can create opportunities for such support and positive input. Much of the counselling support now on offer is confidential and even found outside the hospice or medical setting. Those who are administratively and professionally responsible for carers may not themselves be the best people to offer that special care and support carers need.

As patients we must realise that doctors, relatives and carers have needs too. As patients, we can encourage our carers to take advantage of all the help that is available and this is one crucial way that dying patients can support those who are meant to be supporting them. Carers must also recognise that patients will and do worry about them as carers. Knowing that they will be properly looked after, especially in the bereavement process, will relieve the patient's anxiety. Good doctors and carers must take proper care of themselves. Only thus can they provide the very best care for the dying.

Questions about Care of the Dying

What do I think and feel about my own death?

Have I discussed this with my doctor, family and friends?

Have I made clear what I want and do not want to happen if I am terminally ill?

Have I instructed the doctor if I do not want others to know I am terminally ill?

Have I been to visit a hospice and do I understand the kind of support and care provided there?

Have I been able to discuss my views of life after death if I want to?

Is my pain being properly controlled?

Am I telling the medical and nursing staff about my need for more or less pain relief?

Do I realise the limits of what medicine will be able to do for me?

Have I been able to express my worries about what will happen to those I love after I die?

Am I under pressure from my relatives to go into hospital and have treatment I do not want?

Have I told the doctor about this?

Have I made clear what arrangements I want to happen after my death?

Notes to Chapter 7
1. *Regina* v. *Cox*, Winchester Crown Court (September 1992).

8

SUICIDE AND EUTHANASIA

Since 1961, suicide has no longer been a criminal act. The law was changed not only because it was impossible to take a successful suicide to court, but because few believed that those who were unsuccessful benefited in any way from being charged with a crime. Some folk regard the abolition of suicide as a crime as establishing a right to die. In reality, it rather establishes a freedom. We are free as individuals to end our lives. It can seem like an act of selfishness which does not consider the impact of a suicide on family and friends. Certainly there is a great deal of guilt and concern on the part of those who lose someone by suicide. All regard suicide as a failure either of society to help those of us on the edge of life facing horrendous circumstances or as a failure of someone to cope with whatever they are experiencing.

Doctors are confronted in hospital with people who have attempted to kill themselves. Generally speaking, if someone arrives in an Accident and Emergency Unit, then that seems to indicate they want to be treated. Doctors are obliged to try to preserve life and would try to save the life of an attempted suicide.

The law of the land goes further, for it forbids a doctor and the rest of us from aiding suicide. To aid and abet someone to kill himself or herself is illegal. Doctors are forbidden to give pills for the purpose of taking one's life or instructions on how to commit suicide. A number of years ago a group called EXIT produced a book called *A Guide to Self Deliverance*. It provided detailed information on how to end your life. It was withdrawn because of the law forbidding the aiding of suicide. As patients we are not able to have our doctors provide us with the means of taking our own lives. This will not deter some people from asking the doctor, but patients must be clear that any doctor who does supply information or drugs knowing that these will be used in suicide is liable to be charged.

Changing Perceptions on Euthanasia

Doctors are not only subject to the law concerning assisting suicide, they are also, like the rest of us, subject to laws forbidding murder. From the earliest expression of medical ethics in codes like the Hippocratic Oath, doctors were forbidden to take human life. Doctors are trained to be life preservers. Yet doctors are also obliged to try to alleviate our pain and suffering. This has led to the rise of the hospice movement, where the thrust has been not just on care of the dying, but also in the science of pain relief. One of the effects of some forms of pain relief is that the drugs may not just alleviate our pain. They may also hasten death.

Double effect

Doctors do give people drugs realising that eventually these drugs will hasten the death of the patient. The usual way this process is described is by the law of double effect. When I do something intending to produce a particular effect, like giving someone an injection to alleviate their pain, then it is obvious that I am responsible for what I do and what happens. There are, however, sometimes other effects which might follow a particular action.

My own father suffered from lung cancer. He was in a great deal of pain. In the early sixties the usual way of relieving pain was to give opiate drugs. The problem was these were addictive and meant that as the cancer spread and the pain increased, he needed more and more of the drugs to give relief. As the dosage increased, there came a point where the level of drug he was being given ended his life. How can this be defended by doctors?

In an obvious sense, doctors have to accept responsibility for what they do and all its results. However, the intention is important too. In this case, the aim and intention were quite clearly to alleviate my father's pain. Over a long period of time, he was given drugs to relieve his pain. Pain relief was clearly the intended effect. The increased dosages produced a second or double effect – hastening death. Most doctors accept that this is not only a proper way to treat pain, but is the only way they can act. That pain-killers can hasten death is not because doctors want to kill people, but because medical science cannot yet cure all pain without very nasty, and in this case fatal, side-effects. What makes it plain that the doctor is not trying to kill the patient is two things. The giving of drugs over a period of time where the dose is related directly to the pain relief needed shows the intention of alleviating pain. It must also be the case that if the doctor could give pain relief without having the second or double effect of death, then that would be what he or she intended to happen.

Doctors face a double demand from us as patients. They must not kill us, but they must try all they can to alleviate our pain. On occasions, especially in the past, doctors have sometimes been too aggressive in treating patients. In a sense, some doctors have prolonged the process of dying rather than saved a life. Doctors do have to recognise that death is not to be resisted at all costs and certainly not by every means. Patients may not wish to have their lives preserved. While doctors may not kill patients, even if the patient asks for that, doctors can and do allow patients to die.

Acts and Omissions

There is a difference in the medical world between active steps to kill someone and a clinical judgement to allow someone to die. We often call this letting nature take its course. Some philosophers do not believe that we can distinguish morally between an act and an omission. Doctors disagree not just on psychological grounds. They also describe what happens to make an important and moral distinction. If a doctor gives a patient a fatal injection the patient will die from that injection. The doctor's action kills the patient. That is murder. If a doctor does nothing to a patient and there is nothing wrong with a patient, then nothing will happen because of what the doctor does or does not do. The doctor's omission does not have any effect on a normal healthy person. If the person has a terminal illness and is dying of that illness or of an infection like pneumonia, then the doctor may decide not to treat the infection, and not begin any treatment which would make little or no difference to the outcome. The fact that the doctor omits treatment does not kill the patient. The terminal illness or infection kills the patient. If there was nothing wrong with the patient, the doctor's omission would have no effect. The doctor's omission only has an effect because there is a terminal illness or infection present. Of course, the doctor might delay the process of death and will do that if the patient wants to carry on living. If a patient has had enough suffering and pain and wants to die, then doctors are morally and legally entitled to let the patient die.

Withdrawal of Treatment

As with so much of medical care, there are some very hard cases. People who are in what is called a persistent vegetative state create particular problems, because part of their brain is dead, but they are not brainstem dead. Some of these people are unaware of what is happening to them. They have no sensation or awareness. But they can often breathe by themselves, have periods of wakefulness, and seem to react, even if only in a reflex way. The case of Tony Bland, who was injured in the Hillsborough football disaster, makes the point. He was in a persistent vegetative state for over three years and only kept alive by a feeding tube through his nose which pumped food and antibiotics into his stomach.

The courts decided to withdraw the feeding tube. In legal opinion, artificial feeding by tube or pump is a medical treatment and can be withdrawn at any time, if it is considered to be in the best interests of the patient. The doctors and the Bland family agreed successfully that it was in Tony's best interests to have the tube withdrawn and for him to be allowed to die. Even without 1,500 such cases in the UK, this decision is very important, not least for the financial implications. It cost, in 1992, £60,000 a year to keep people like Tony Bland alive. This is not the place to debate whether giving food artificially is or is not really a medical treatment or whether it can ever be in someone's best interests to die. What matters for us as potential patients and families of patients is what we can expect from doctors.

Doctors have been instructed that they may only withdraw artificial feeding and hydration with the explicit permission of the courts. It is not up to the family or the doctors on their own. If we do not want to be fed in that kind of way, then we should leave clear written instructions that this is what we wish to happen. Doctors will do exactly what we want. But I have to confess to some unease about this decision, not just because of views of sanctity of life, or from a fear of a slippery slope which might allow euthanasia to creep in. The key issue is withdrawal of treatment and whether or not it is more like an act or an omission. Doctors tend to regard withdrawal of treatment as an omission and the law generally supports them.

To explain my hesitation I usually use the parallel between a building which is in danger of collapsing and a terminally ill patient. If I decide to knock the building down or kill the patient, I commit an act, which is murder. If I decide to do nothing – to opt for an omission – then the building will collapse, but it collapses in its own time, because it is a collapsing building. Similarly, a terminally ill person will die if I omit to intervene in the situation, but they die because of terminal illness and not because of my omission. If I decide to support the collapsing building and put in a prop to hold it up, the building will survive because I am supporting it. It may even come to depend on the support and prop, so that it cannot survive without it. In the same way, the terminally ill person may come to depend on the food being given by a nasal tube. If I then change my mind and decide to remove the support system, the building collapses, the patient dies. That collapse and death happen at that time because of what I have done. I withdrew the support and killed the patient or the building. It is true that the building was collapsing and that the patient was terminally ill. Both would have come to an end at some time. They came to an end when they did because of what I did. So, in my own mind, withdrawing treatment is more like a positive act than an omission.

The Right to Die, Autonomy and Dignity

As patients we do not have a right to die, but we do have a freedom to take our own life and can request that doctors allow us to die. What we do not have is a right to be killed. As free and autonomous people we can decide what we want to happen to us, but we cannot expect or require someone else to be forced to act against the law and their conscience. The Voluntary Euthanasia Society is in favour of patients being allowed to die with dignity and argues for a change in the law to allow doctors to end life. They point to the way that Holland has moved. Euthanasia was permitted in Holland. Now it is becoming legal. If someone is terminally ill and wishes to be killed, then they are interviewed by doctors. These doctors must ensure that the person is terminally ill and has a fixed and consistent desire to die. The doctors then report to the police that they intend to perform an act of 'mercy-killing' on a particular date. Once this act has been done, they report that fact to the police. This is to allow the police the opportunity to examine the case, if they so wish. Usually this does not happen. In February of 1993, the Dutch parliament moved to make euthanasia a legal possibility.

One basic argument is that individuals should be free to do whatever they want with their own bodies. Part of what it means to be a member of society is that our rights and freedoms are restricted. We are not free and able to do whatever we want. We are forced to wear seat-belts in cars, helmets if we ride motor bikes, and are not free to do anything and everything. As we noted earlier, we are now free to take our own lives. Society and the law of the land do not allow us to involve someone else in ending our life.

All of us want to die with dignity, and many of us feel deeply uneasy about the prospect of being older, more dependent on other people, losing our independence and our ability, and slowly deteriorating in body and mind. What we are able to do and how we are able to live will depend on what is possible and appropriate at different ages and stages of life. Certainly, how we live at eighty is not the same as life in our twenties. This does not seem itself like a loss of dignity.

Many feel that only individuals are able to judge their own level of dignity and what they are happy to live with. Much of our sense of self-worth does arise from how we feel about ourselves. Dignity can be given by others to us. Those who are helpless and totally dependent can be given a great deal of dignity by the way the rest of us treat them. Hospital and nursing-home staff are often wonderful in that respect, in the care and dignity they give as they look after us when we are totally dependent on others.

It is true that as we grow older we become more of a burden in terms of health care. In a society where there is a growing number of the elderly, there might arise pressure to 'get rid of' those who do not contribute very much to society. It is deeply offensive to say that older people do not contribute to society. They certainly have contributed a great deal throughout their lives, not least in paying to support the National Health Service. Society owes a great obligation to those who have worked and served us faithfully. If they are now more dependent on the rest of us, we should share that load gladly. Pressure can arise, though, from the older person himself or herself. There is a pride which refuses to be dependent or to take what is often regarded as 'charity' rather than a right, and a desire to maintain independence. All this must be respected, but is not an excuse for failing to care for the old and in no way justifies a call to 'solve' the problems of ageing by euthanasia.

Compassion

Perhaps the strongest argument for euthanasia relates to compassion. You would not let an animal suffer in the way you let human beings suffer. We put animals out of their misery, and should be willing to do the same for human beings. This sounds reasonable until we look at the two assumptions such statements make. It assumes human beings are the same as animals. They are not, and we should treat human beings and human life with even more care than we do animal life. It also assumes that there is no alternative to a painful death and misery. This is not true. As we saw in the Chapter on Care of the Dying, there is genuine pain relief available for most of our pain. There is psychological, personal and spiritual support in organisations like the Hospice Movement. Such a movement enables true compassion. Compassionate doctors kill pain and not the patients. Good medicine seeks to find yet more adequate and total pain relief rather than to take an easy way out by ending patients' lives.

The Sanctity of Life

Religious and non-religious people alike accept the fundamental principle of the sanctity of life. This does not mean we must try to preserve life at all costs, but it does mean that any taking of life is a serious business and requires justification. We train doctors to act to preserve life and that is deeply embedded in their personal and professional consciences.

Society does, however, permit justified killing in certain circumstances. In war and capital punishment, societies justify the taking of human life. It is extremely hard to see in either of these situations that life is being ended for the benefit of the individual being killed. That seems equally true in most abortion cases. It is for the benefit of someone else, rather than the fetus, that life is being taken. The law justifies that taking of life. There are some cases of abortion where it is alleged to be for the benefit of the fetus. Where there is severe abnormality or handicap, or even a possibility of these problems, abortions are performed on the grounds that it is in the best interests of the fetus. That life is considered to be not worth living.

This seems the nearest ground to finding a way of justifying the taking of life. If someone feels that life is not worth living and if society agrees, then has society the responsibility to end that life? It is extremely difficult for any of us to judge that someone else's life is worthless. It is also a very subjective judgement to make about our own life and may ignore what others feel about our worth and dignity. Even if it is true, that in itself does not justify us in killing people, if we believe that killing other people is wrong, or only justified in extreme situations. The practical dangers become important in looking at such a stance.

Practical Problems

The unease about euthanasia and any law permitting it rests not just on the principle of the sanctity of life but on practical problems. There are too many to list fully, but the main concerns rest on the role of doctors, valid consent, insurance and inheritance, and the fear of a slippery slope in the taking of life.

Living wills

Doctors are seen as life preservers. We expect them to struggle to save life. We recognise that sometimes they try too hard and for too long to keep life going. If we were to change that role and instead make or allow doctors to become death controllers, many feel that the fundamental role of trust and confidence between a patient and the doctor would be at risk and break down. If we knew doctors killed, then we might be more than a little worried if they were giving us an injection to put us to sleep 'for a little while'. This is probably the argument which most concerns the British Medical Association. The BMA produced a report on euthanasia in 1988, which rejects it as an option for doctors. Euthanasia legislation would fundamentally and irrevocably alter the relationship between doctors and patients.

Instead the BMA are in favour of advanced directives (often called 'living wills') as an expression of what the patient wants a doctor *not* to do. These directives make it clear that a patient does not want certain kinds of treatment under specific circumstances, like a serious and major accident or stroke. Doctors do not feel absolutely bound by such directives because they are only too well aware that medicine is constantly changing and new discoveries and improvements are being made all the time. They are also concerned with valid consent.

Pressure to give consent

In any euthanasia legislation, a key area would be valid consent. Have patients been given and grasped all the relevant information about their situation and the likely development of their disease, and are they free from pressure to have euthanasia? Even if we can be sure about the giving and receiving of information, though that is hard where medicine is changing and improving, then it is hard to know that there was no undue pressure on a person to agree to euthanasia. It is vital that we as patients are able to change our minds even in the midst of treatment. It is not possible to change our minds once we have been killed. It is also extremely difficult to see how we could check that someone is really better off being dead than alive. We cannot wake them up and ask them. Framing safeguards to protect the vulnerable in society is vital. The elderly, the confused, the handicapped might all too easily be pressurised by families to have their lives ended.

Inheritance

This leads clearly to problems over inheritance. If granny has a house worth £200,000 and is confused, then I might be tempted to solve any financial problems by 'encouraging' granny to have euthanasia, if it were legal. She might easily be brought to feel that she had

had a 'good innings', would lose her dignity and would be better off dead. Ensuring that all of us patients were protected from those who might gain from our deaths is very difficult to guarantee.

Euthanasia – no easy solution

The slippery slope argument rests on the idea that if we give people an inch they take a mile. If we allow euthanasia in a voluntary way for the terminally ill, then we will slide to a situation where we are willing to end the life of the 'unacceptable', 'worthless' and 'burdensome' even in a compulsory way. It can sound far-fetched. We begin with voluntary euthanasia and end up with the gas chambers in Nazi Germany. Some reply that there is no necessity to slide down the slope. All we have to do is draw an absolute line and make sure no one goes beyond that line. The problem is that we have seen that when 'justified' killing was allowed in the Abortion Act of 1967, what began as giving doctors *permission* to perform abortions under limited circumstances has become an *expectation* of abortion on demand, and that many doctors feel that there is almost a *requirement* to perform abortions. Behind the fear of the slippery slope is a pessimism about human nature. We have special limits and these are meant to be absolute lines and obeyed.

In practice, many people drive above the speed limit. They do not see the standard as absolute, but rather try to get away with as much as possible. Often human nature takes advantage of others if they are vulnerable and it is to be for our benefit.

Current Legislation

As stated earlier in the chapter, suicide is no longer a crime, but it remains an offence to help someone commit suicide. The penalty can be up to fourteen years in prison. The law against taking life was interpreted by Devlin in a case where a fatal dose was administered to a patient. Devlin stressed that a doctor should do all he or she could to relieve pain and suffering even if there was an incidental shortening of life.[1] The recent Cox case stressed the illegality of acting where the intention was to kill and thus alleviate pain. This is quite different from alleviating pain and inevitably hastening death because of the limits of pain relief.[2]

The debate goes on

Different people will have different views about suicide and euthanasia. They will also disagree about whether or not to change the law of the land. The experience of Holland will give us increasing information about the danger and extent of the abuse of euthanasia and its effects. Currently it seems that it has led to a much wider killing of people outside the regulated euthanasia system and deep fear and unease among those in institutions about what will happen to them.[3] We, as patients, and as citizens, need to look at the arguments very carefully and decide not just what is best for us as individuals, but what is best for the whole of society.

Notes to Chapter 8
1. *R* v. *Adams* (*The Times*, 9 April 1957).
2. *Regina* v. *Cox*, Winchester Crown Court (September 1992).
3. 'Elderly Persons on the subject of Euthanasia' in J.H. Segers, *Issues in Law and Medicine* (1988) 3, 429–37.

9

THE WIDER ROLES OF DOCTORS

The history of codes of medical ethics is full of details of doctors' relationships with each other. At times this has seemed to be more important than the doctor's relationship with his or her patients. In recent times that emphasis on inter-professional responsibilities has changed, but it remains important to doctors. It also matters to us as patients, for the way that doctors relate to each other, the wider world and to people who have some kind of authority over them, like employers, does fundamentally affect the partnership between patients and doctors. We patients need to be aware of the kinds of pressures, demands and duties doctors have to people other than patients and what kind of impact that might have on the treatment and care of patients, our confidentiality and autonomy and our choices. If a doctor has business interests and a financial aspect is involved that affects what the doctor might prescribe or what treatment might be recommended, then we have the right to know that this is the case. Doctors must be honest with us as patients when financial matters may affect our treatment or options for treatment.

Most doctors are employed by the National Health Service, Trusts or local authorities, or are in private practice. There are some doctors who are employed by companies or businesses. There are doctors working in the armed forces, the prison service, and some employed by the police. At various times, a doctor may act on behalf of an insurance company or prospective employer. Doctors are not entirely free agents. They are answerable to the General Medical Council and have certain legal responsibilities. All these different relationships may have serious effects on patients and their rights and choices.

Insurance and Job Applications

It is not uncommon for insurance companies and prospective employers to require a medical examination or a medical history from applicants. Patients may enter into formal contracts with such companies and have to give formal permission to allow a company to approach the patient's doctor. There is no obligation on a patient to undergo such an examination or to permit the release of private information. Of course, they may not then get the job or the insurance cover they are applying for, so patients are under pressure to accept these steps. It seems quite fair that companies need to know what kind of risk they are taking in employing or insuring a person. None of us can rely on absolute truth-telling from applicants, so the third party – the doctor – will be asked to give medical details which provide a check on information given by the patient and an objective picture of the health and likely medical problems of applicants. The release of information or giving of a medical report cannot be done without the specific permission of the patient. Insurance companies have a responsibility to their other clients to protect their interests. It is clearly not in their best interests to take on people who are known to be high risk or are already seriously ill. In the same way an employer needs to know whether or not an employee or prospective employee is fit for work and has any particular tendencies which might create problems in the workplace. One of the problems for a GP or other doctor who is asked to act on behalf of companies and, in that way, is not acting simply in the best interests of the patient, is that patients might withhold information from the doctor which they know would prejudice their chances of a job or insurance policy. While this is understandable, it destroys the partnership between doctor and patient and puts the doctor at a severe disadvantage as he or she tries to care for the patient. Conflicts of duties and responsibilities can arise for doctors and for patients.

Tests for HIV

Prospective applicants may be encouraged by the body to whom they are applying to have an HIV test. From the doctor's point of view there may be good reasons why a particular patient would not benefit from that testing at that time. The doctor's role is to protect the best interests of a patient, and therefore doctors would need to counsel patients and warn them of any social or personal harm that might result. As a side issue, patients need to be assured that they are not at risk from doctors who may be HIV positive. This will be explored further on page 182. Part of the problem for patients and doctors is that while someone may be HIV positive, that does not mean that they are not fit to do most jobs. How widely that is understood and accepted by others may create a problem for the doctor, who, knowing the likely misunderstanding, may feel it is better for an individual patient if that information is not given. Doctors may be faced with a stark dilemma: either to tell the truth and lead to injustice, or be economical with the truth to let justice prevail and protect the patient.

In completing forms for insurance and employment purposes, doctors will often be asked to speculate on the lifestyles of patients and whether or not they engage in high-risk activities. Such information is not a medical matter and may be entirely the result of subjective judgements on the part of the doctor. Questions about how much a person smokes, their level of sexual activity, and the possible abuse of drugs may not be part of a doctor's medical care of a patient. Such information may be gleaned from contact and interviews with patients, but it was not part of the medical information required to deal with specific medical problems. The doctor may have acquired such information by accident. The patient would not expect the doctor to note or remember it, far less use it in replying to company requests for information. Doctors are in the business of giving factual, relevant medical information and not speculation, however well-founded that speculation might be. It is the job of the insurance or employing company to measure and assess risks and the other implications of that medical information. Doctors must beware of a slide to speculate and to offer their own interpretations rather than the mere facts. We patients need to be aware of the pressure on doctors to jump to conclusions and then recount these to others.

Medical records

We patients can always ask for an independent doctor if there is any concern that our own doctor may put us in a difficult and unsuccessful position. Normally, most of us as patients do not even consider such a step. It is enough for us to know that our interests are safeguarded because medical information about us can only be released with our consent. The right of access to one's own medical records – as stated in the Access to Medical Reports Act 1988 – is important here.

These records may contain wrong information or material which is irrelevant and not medical at all. In giving written permission for a doctor to reveal information, we must realise that all such information may be passed on. We as patients must bear this in mind and should know exactly what is contained in our file.

Doctors who are not usually dealing with a particular patient may discover something which the patient and his or her doctor need to know. That should be checked with the patient and permission obtained to inform the GP. For a GP who is acting in a dual role for the patient and the company, then he or she should make it clear to a patient if there is any material or information which might be harmful if it were disclosed.

Doctors have a responsibility to keep information about patients confidential. In job or insurance applications, the patient is giving permission to break that confidentiality. Once information has been sent to a company, and that means being sent to the medical person in that company, the problem of confidentiality is that other people may have to have access to that information who are not bound by the professional codes of doctors. This is part of the price employees pay to be employed or insured. That in no way detracts from the responsibility of doctors within companies to maximise the confidentiality and privacy of individuals. Proper business practice and good ethical standards will help, but we must be aware that information about us will become widely available once we make job or insurance applications. We patients are free to make a choice about applying or not, and the doctor's responsibility is to help us realise the implications and consequences of such choices. Some of that information is necessary for people like employers, who need to protect other people in the workplace. They may also need to protect us as patients and avoid putting us at risk. Disclosure of medical information can be for the benefit of the doctor's particular patient and for other employees in that situation.

Disclosing genetic information

In insurance matters there is an increasing trend to try to discover genetic information about people. As it becomes more likely that much of the cause of disease and the development of particular diseases depends on one's genetic background and make-up, companies will want to know that history. This raises two problems. The first is that simply because people have a genetic predisposition towards a disease does not guarantee that they will develop it. There are many other factors involved. The second problem is that companies may not know what significance such information may have and make false and wrong judgements and decisions based on misunderstandings. The giving of such information might breach a patient's rights in another way. A particular patient might have decided that he or she does not want to know about the risk of a genetic disease or even to know that genetic information. It may be recorded in the medical notes for the benefit of other doctors as and when they are involved in the treatment of that patient. Companies might want to know and benefit from knowing that information. The doctor ought not to break that confidentiality without the permission of the patient and should make it clear what significance there might be for the patient if that information were known by companies.

Doctors Fully Employed by Companies

Doctors may be fully employed by a company to care for their employees. Their concerns will be with the health and safety of workers as well as the safety of the work setting and conditions of work. In emergencies they will be expected to provide immediate medical care and arrange for the transfer of patients to hospital or the care of the patient's own GP. They may also play a role in the health and safety education of people within a particular workplace. Industrial or business settings can provide an excellent base for research into work-related stress, injury and health promotion. Many of the advances in rehabilitation have arisen from those involved in these kinds of settings and their insights have been then transferred to help handicapped people.

Part of the normal responsibilities of such doctors will be regular medical examination of people who drive public vehicles or lorries, as well as of those who are sick or returning to work. In this way, some of the work normally done by GPs can be completed by an occupational health doctor. This will involve some contact with the GP to ensure that a patient is properly cared for and not given conflicting advice. Doctors should try to ensure good communication with each other, especially in the handing over of a patient to a hospital or GP after some incident at work. In all these aspects of medical care in the workplace, a patient's consent must be obtained. Doctors must make sure that patients know the reason for any medical examination or procedure. Patients must also give consent for any contact with their own GPs and for the transfer of information to the employer. Those who employ others have a right to know if there is a risk to or from one of their staff. They do not have a right to know specific medical details or any information which is not directly relevant to the health and safety of the patient or others. How long someone will be off work, whether they are fit to do their previous job, what degree of risk there is of recurrence and of continuing disability and what pattern future absences might take, are all relevant to employers who may have to decide to terminate someone's contract or job on the grounds of ill health. All of this information should only be divulged by a doctor to an employer on a need-to-know basis. It is important that the doctor also tries to make sure that an employer understands the significance of that information and does not misunderstand it.

Much of this material will be recorded. These records are the property of the doctor who has responsibility for employees' health. When a doctor leaves, that information should remain in the hands of a doctor or nurse who takes over that responsibility. If no medically suitable person is available, then the records should be destroyed. It is important that patients are able to trust doctors in industrial and business settings. The keeping confidential of medical information is an important plank in maintaining that trust. Where other staff are involved in handling such sensitive information, they should be expected to abide by the general rules of confidentiality. In the event of an inquiry into an accident or incident at work, then patients should be asked to give consent to any relevant records being given to all the sides in the dispute. Only the law can require a doctor to reveal information without the express permission of the patient.

Only in the case of danger to others must that rule of confidentiality
be set aside for the sake of others.

Employees and random drug tests

Doctors are in the business of health promotion and disease prevention. They are responsible for the whole workforce. One relatively
recent move on the part of some companies to identify possible
risk areas and people, is random drug and alcohol testing. My
son works part-time for a large grocery chain. All employees are
subject to random searches to prevent stealing. When they take
the job that is made clear as part of the job of working for that
company. Likewise, if random drug testing is to be used, then this
should be known and accepted by the employee when he or she joins
the company or the new policy is introduced. The information gained
should only be used for the specific reason given by the company.
Doctors must protect the rights of patients and ensure that no other
use is made of that information.

Pilots, drivers of public service and heavy goods vehicles, and
people like miners, doctors and atomic industry workers may require
regular check-ups, and the results of these may mean that they are
no longer able to continue in their current post. We patients must
recognise that doctors are there to provide medical information and
not to make decisions about employment or its termination. Doctors
do have a responsibility to give relevant information about health
problems and risks, but this should be done with the patient's
consent. That consent should be gained before the examination or
testing. It is part of the special partnership between patients and
doctors in industrial and business settings.

It is not only information about individual patients which a doctor
learns. Information about the workplace and management practices
will also come to light. This may create a problem for the doctor.
He may try unsuccessfully to persuade a company to change bad
work practices which create dangers for the workers and for the
public. The management may refuse to listen and to make the
necessary safety changes. In such a situation the doctor should tell
the employer what will be done. It is the doctor's duty to protect
patients. If responsibility for others means warning them of risk in
the work setting then the doctor must speak up and accept the

consequences. This is hard, not least within the medical world. Doctors and nurses who blow the whistle on work practices which create danger for others are not always popular with colleagues, far less with those who employ them. Nevertheless, doctors have a moral responsibility, and if their conscience tells them that something is wrong and they have exhausted all proper channels to put that right, then whistle-blowing may be the last resort.[1]

Doctors in Public Health Roles

The same kind of whistle-blowing can be an issue for those doctors who are responsible for the care and welfare of the general public. Their responsibilities cover the care and services available from local authorities. To do their job will mean close contact with the community at every level and involve speaking and advising on issues that concern public health. They may be faced with a conflict between the concern for the individual and that for the community as a whole.

To protect babies, we have them immunised. The long-term effect of immunisation is to prevent the spread of particular diseases. The incidence of polio has been much reduced by the use of the polio vaccine. However, some people do react to immunisation. A very small percentage of babies will have serious problems from such injections. Parents have to decide whether the risk from the disease or from the immunisation is greater. Most of us are quite clear that the benefit of having the injection far outweighs the small risk. But if a parent decides the opposite, then there is a risk of such disease spreading not only to the child but to other people. Society does not force this kind of treatment on patients. Consent and autonomy are still the key with patient choice controlling. There may arise circumstances where that autonomy has to be limited because of the risks to others. In the case of a notifiable disease then the local authority is required to act to protect others. That may mean the removal of a patient to a place of safety not just for himself or herself but also for others. Public screening needs to be carefully explained to folk who are not yet patients. The purpose of such information and its uses must be clear so that people may give an informed and proper consent to take part in such screening.

Public health officials are bound by the law and given certain powers by that law to remove people who are at risk or posing a threat to the well-being of others. This may include the elderly, and people suffering from dementia or mental disorder. The legal basis for this is examined below.

Doctors in Legal Settings

Doctors are sometimes employed on a temporary or permanent basis to work with and for the police or in prisons. Such roles can all too easily create professional and moral conflicts. Both those suspected of crimes and those found guilty and the victims of crimes may fall into the care of doctors. The main element which provides assurance for patients is that doctors will not proceed without consent. Ideally, that consent should be in a written form and witnessed. Patients must be free, wherever possible, to choose which doctor will examine them. They must know why they are being examined and the purpose of any test or sample taken. Where a crime is involved, patients must realise that confidentiality is not a total or absolute privilege. What is discovered may be taken and used in evidence against the person at some later stage.

Those who have been victims of crime require sensitive handling. They are being examined not for their own good, but in order to provide evidence of a crime. That examination may have to take place immediately after a harrowing event like rape. Patients will require careful counselling and support as they are subjected to further indignity. They have the right to refuse to be examined and doctors must not create undue pressure, but explain what will happen if they are unwilling to provide the necessary evidence. In the case of children, the confused elderly or the mentally disordered, consent may be obtained from someone else. No adult victim who is competent can be forced to have a medical examination. No doctor should be involved in medical procedures if a victim patient refuses to give consent. Victims also have the right to choose to be examined by a doctor of the same sex or their own GP if that is their wish.

When it comes to those who are suspected of crimes, then doctors should seek consent before examining them. If someone refuses, for example in the case of a suspected drink-driving offence, then that refusal will lead to an automatic conviction. Any test or examination done must only be used for the specific purpose and criminal charge in question. Conducting an intimate body search may be necessary if there is some realistic possibility that drugs may have been concealed in the rectal or other private parts of the body, according to the Police and Criminal Evidence Act 1984. The increasing use of DNA fingerprinting using small samples of blood, hair, semen or other body fluids should be carried out with written consent and only for the specific charges at issue.

Care while in custody

When people are in custody they automatically lose privacy. Police officers may be present at examinations. It is important that they should be of the same sex, if the examination is intimate. Doctors too may need to be protected from aggressive patients who resent what is happening. If the person is under seventeen then a relative or parent must be present and give consent. When dealing with children, both the consent of the child and of the parents should be obtained before an examination or sample is taken.

Complaints about mistreatment in custody require care, and patients need to know that if they make such a complaint then there is no automatic right to see the results of any examination done to establish evidence of abuse or violence.

In prison settings many of the same issues arise, but for doctors in such settings there are other responsibilities to those in authority, particularly to the governor. Prisoners who are patients have suffered not only the loss of their liberty, but also of some aspects of their autonomy. Their choices are limited. But they have not lost the right to good health care and treatment. There should be no pressure on a prisoner to receive treatment. Drugs ought not to be used to control difficult patients. Both of these responses to patients would be wrong. While on remand, patients are free to consult their own GP rather than the prison doctor, and that consultation may take place in private without a guard present. For those serving a sentence those freedoms are withdrawn. These issues are discussed in the British Medical Association's report 'Health Care of Remand Prisoners', published in 1990.

In terms of confidentiality, the consent of the patient to sharing information should be part of good practice. There will inevitably be cases where a patient will refuse to permit disclosure of information. The doctor has a responsibility to the governor, the staff and other prisoners as well as to the patient. If in the doctor's judgement it is necessary to break confidentiality in the interests of security and safety, that may be done and will have to be justified. Medical information should only be noted in the medical record and not the prison record of a patient. The prison authorities only need to know a patient's medical condition in respect of fitness to work or for staff management concerns. Any contact with the prison patient's GP should be with the explicit consent of the patient. Only the best interests of the patient would be considered a sufficient ground for overturning that general rule. Patients should be aware that GPs may charge a prison service for such work and this might cause a delay in the receipt of the information.

The role of prison doctors

Doctors in prison have a dual responsibility. They are to care for and protect the well-being of their patients and they are answerable to the governor for the security and safety of the health of prisoners and staff. In Northern Ireland, the particular community problems there have led to a clear separation of the clinical and prison roles. The genuine independence of medical care is not simply being ensured, it is also being seen to be ensured. Doctors in that setting face issues involved in terrorism and in particular hunger strikes. Some patients have decided to make their protest on a variety of issues by starving themselves to death. To oppose this by force-feeding would contravene the rights of the individual unless there were obvious clinical grounds to intervene. These might be if the patient were incompetent to make such a decision or some undue pressure or coercion was forcing the prisoner to act in that way. If a prisoner is firmly resolved to die then a doctor must allow that after full counselling and persuasion to change his or her mind. The doctor should not attempt to resuscitate such a patient if the patient is consistent in the desire to die and realises that there may be heart failure.[2]

More generally, prison doctors may have to blow the whistle on prison conditions and authorities who refuse to listen to representations or to change situations where the health and rights of prisoners are being abused. This is an extreme step and there are many other ways of confronting the inadequacies of the prison setting and system. Prison patients are particularly at risk from suicide and doctors should be extra vigilant about warning signs and alert to help patients at risk. Complaints against staff are made and the doctor must not simply side with the staff, but offer objective medical and factual judgement about the evidence of abuse shown by physical or psychological examination. Dealing with the mentally ill in prisons is a difficult matter. Medical staff are not always well qualified and should refer to more expert medical advice when such problems arise, in accordance with the Mental Health Acts of 1983 and 1984.

Prisons are unhealthy places and have a high proportion of unhealthy people. Doctors must try to safeguard those who are at risk not simply from disease but from the abuse of their rights, autonomies and respect.

Doctors in Government Services

Doctors may be called on to give expert witness in criminal and civil proceedings and to make a medical assessment of people who are applying for asylum. There is a Medical Foundation for the Care of Victims of Torture that offers advice and guidance in such cases. Doctors are meant to be impartial and objective. They must not go beyond the facts and begin to speculate or interpret. It is wrong for doctors to withhold vital information if they are asked for it and it is relevant to the court. Their answers should be factual, detailed, carefully worded and make no unsubstantiated assertions. Doctors in the armed forces have similar dual responsibilities to doctors in prison. The only additional problem may arise because of the medical care of families of those in the Services. It may be in the best interests of a community that some matter of medical importance be revealed, even though the confidentiality of the family might be broken. Such cases should be rare, but patients may not have a genuine choice of which doctor they wish to see, and must realise that the doctor may have to report the result, though not the content, of a medical consultation to a superior officer. This step must only be taken in the best interests of people as a whole and not just to avoid offending other officers or the relevant authorities.

The General Medical Council

Doctors are regulated by the GMC, not only in relation to dealing with patients, but also in their relationships with other doctors. A doctor who falls foul of the high professional and moral standards expected of doctors can be charged with 'serious professional misconduct'. The GMC is responsible for disciplining doctors. This has tended to concentrate on professional issues and been very weak on dealing with poor standards of training and mistakes. Now there is much greater scrutiny of the way that illness may be affecting the performance of doctors and the specific details of their prescribing patterns, lack of medical-record keeping and failure to see patients when required. It is clear that society as a whole expects higher standards from doctors than from the rest of us. That may well seem unfair and unjust. In an obvious way it is both of those, but it is also an expression of the privileged position doctors enjoy in their relationships with patients, the vulnerability of such patients and the need for doctors to be monitored.

Part of such monitoring should include awareness of limitations. Often, through lack of experience and proper training, doctors may put patients at risk. The horrendous hours worked by junior doctors are a good example where patients may suffer. The career pressure can make doctors refuse to admit to their lack of knowledge. Good training and supervision are the ways to protect patients. If a doctor is in doubt he or she should refer the patient to a more senior or specialised doctor.

Patients should also be referred when a doctor is unwilling to meet their needs on some moral ground. In contraceptive, abortion, or drug-related issues, patients may not receive particular treatments from their own GP. If that refusal rests on a moral disagreement, then the patient is entitled to be referred speedily to another doctor, who should be informed of all the necessary information. Communication between doctors is vital if patients are to be well served and protected. One doctor must accept responsibility for the overall care of a patient. It should be clear to the patient who that doctor is. When a GP refers a patient to a specialist, the patient should be told why that is happening and why that specialist has been chosen. Patients should be free to seek another opinion. If a specialist is contacted by a patient without a referral from a GP, then many will not accept that patient. If they do, it is normal practice to inform the GP of the situation and that the specialist is taking over responsibility at the request of the patient. In situations where a patient is moving from one area – for example, a hospital, prison or home – to the care of another doctor, good levels of communication are vital. The patient should be directly involved in consenting to that information and care being transferred and the patient should be given as much choice as possible.

Doctors in conflict

Doctors can and do disagree with one another. It can happen in the dissolution of a medical practice and over practice rules and guidelines. In all this the patients' well-being must be protected. Doctors are often in the best position to know exactly when another doctor is failing in his or her responsibility to patients. There are and must be limits to the loyalties of doctors to each other for the sake of loyalty to patients and their best interests. Such limits are inadequate care, sexual impropriety, alcohol or drug abuse. Doctors should try to persuade colleagues to seek professional help, but if that fails then doctors must inform the relevant authorities for the sake of the patients who may be at risk.

In some of the new Trusts there is a secrecy clause which is part of the doctor's contract. It forbids making public sensitive information about the Trust and things pertaining to its work. This might constitute a very serious attack on the freedom of doctors to express their concerns publicly to prevent harm to patients. Commercial interest should not affect the safety of patients.[3] Similar problems can arise in closed institutions where the public are not able to go freely. In such settings the welfare of patients is even more the responsibility of the doctors there. Sadly, it is often the nursing staff who have acted as the patient's advocate.

In the creation and dissolution of a general practice, patients must be protected by ensuring that areas where disputes may arise are properly agreed and a reconciliation process for the resolving of disputes is in place. The BMA provides such an arbitration service and has local bodies to help doctors with such problems. The areas most susceptible to dispute cover finance, duties and responsibilities, time off, the mechanism for consultation, the general practice approach and philosophy towards patients, research on patients, the use of chaperones for intimate examinations and arrangements for the ending of a practice. If a dispute arises, the care of us as patients, our freedom to choose our own doctor, and the safeguarding of patient confidentiality and records are paramount.

The Effects of New NHS Funding

Changes in the funding of the NHS have made differences to doctors' relationships with patients. Doctors do not simply provide medical care and treatment, they are also in the business of preventing disease and promoting good health. To facilitate these aims the Government has set targets for the number of people who should have smear tests and immunisation. Previously these were recommended by a doctor because he or she believed that a patient would benefit from them. Now there may arise a doubt in a patient's mind. If a doctor is only one short of the target set, then a major financial loss will occur not just for the doctor but for the practice. The doctor has every incentive therefore to ensure that targets are met. The problem is that a patient may not be very keen to have a particular test or jab, yet be pressurised into having it. Even when the doctor is acting in perfectly good faith, there may still be a doubt in the patient's mind. Any screening of patients should only be done with their consent, and that will mean an explanation of why the screening is necessary and what will be done with the information gleaned. Some doctors are not convinced that such screening is scientifically valid. They are also concerned that it may create a false sense of security for patients, who may feel that there is nothing wrong with them. It may also create an awareness of a disease where there may be no treatment available.

GPs have been encouraged to become fund-holders by the Government. Each practice will receive funds from central Government and will be responsible for setting and maintaining its own budget. This has led to a fear, by doctors and patients, that a two-tier system would be created. There are some glaring examples where some authorities have run out of cash and their patients have not been able to receive the treatment they need. Those authorities with cash can choose to send patients to areas where there is treatment available. The nonsense can then arise of a patient having to travel great distances for treatment, while the local hospital has been too efficient in treating its numbers and has been forced to close down some wards because targets have already been met.

GPs Advertising their Services

If GPs have a financial interest in a pharmacy, nursing home or alternative therapy business and recommend it to a patient, it must be made clear that there is such an interest. Doctors are never justified in pressurising patients to opt for such services unless it is genuinely in the patient's interests. GPs are entitled to advertise their services but under the rules of the GMC. If primary care is being provided it can be advertised, whereas specialist services like vasectomies and hormone replacement therapies cannot. If adverts are placed in the media, they must only be factual and cannot make comparative claims for excellence. This is to limit commercialism and competition between doctors.

The main vehicle for advertising services will be the practice booklet. In many ways this is parallel to the production of a prospectus by each school. Each general practice must produce such a booklet. It should contain details about the doctors, the practice, appointments, home visits, repeat prescriptions and emergencies. It should make clear if contraceptive advice, minor surgery or complementary therapies are available. There must be no advertising which implies some kind of medical approval of facilities which may be health-related such as nursing homes. These booklets can be distributed in the locality, but no telephoning or pressure to join a practice is permitted. The key is the provision of accurate unbiased information to allow patients to make genuinely free and informed choices about medical services and doctors.

Dealing with Sick Doctors

Doctors are advised not to treat themselves or their families. Doctors, like the rest of us, are very good at giving other people advice and not so good at following it themselves. The general level of health care among professional doctors is poor. Doctors are entitled to the same protection of confidentiality when they are ill as the rest of us. There is a national counselling service available for doctors who may need help and the GMC has a voluntary procedure to help doctors who are having problems with alcohol, drugs or mental disorder. Doctors have a responsibility to help each other at the same time as protecting patients.

Doctors who are HIV positive are a particular concern for patients. It is in the public interest to make sure that patients are protected. Doctors are advised to seek medical help if they are aware of such a problem and instructed not to continue to practise medicine if there is any risk at all to patients. Sadly, other doctors may have to ensure that this does happen. Until the public sees that doctors are themselves acting responsibly, such unease will remain. Equality for patients also implies equality for doctors. They are entitled to the same confidentiality as anyone else, but have to recognise that their role in society may put others at risk in ways that are not so for the rest of us.

Dealing with Other Professional Groups

Doctors have always shared responsibility with others for the care of patients. Nurses in particular have long been seen as the 'handmaids' of doctors. Such a term reveals a great deal about the dominance of the medical profession. That dominance has been altering under twin pressures. Increased consumer choice has forced doctors to realise that patients will not tolerate high-handed treatment from doctors. There is also a level of disillusionment among many patients with scientific medicine and a move to trying out alternative therapies. Certainly nurses have often been more concerned with the day-to-day care of patients and have developed a very positive image among the general public. At the same time, the nursing profession has been moving to a more academic disciplinary base. In terms of educational entry, registration, regulation, and a disciplinary process, nurses have attained the kinds of elements which are crucial in professional recognition. This is clearly in addition to the excellent quality of contribution nurses have made to patient care and well-being. Nurses have been able to give doctors insight and background detail which have affected treatment and relationships with the patient. Doctors are increasingly giving nurses the status they deserve.

With changes in Governmental policy there has also been a shift towards more patient care taking place in the community. For this to function properly, there needs to be close liaison and the creation of care teams. Multi-disciplinary teamwork where each member of the team makes a unique contribution is very common. For a team to work well there must be mutual trust, honesty and excellent communication. While doctors may be the leaders of such teams and ultimately responsible for the overall care and management of each patient, each team member provides an important contribution for patients. Part of the increasing professionalism of paramedical groups is their taking responsibility for their own work, according to the Professions Supplementary to Medicine Act 1960.

A professional person is responsible for an awareness of their own limits in knowledge and skill. When that limit is reached, help should be looked for from more experienced or senior folk. Nurses must leave some treatments and decisions to doctors. Nurses do remain responsible for what they do when so instructed by a doctor. If a doctor prescribes too high a dose of a drug for a patient, the nurse must question that dosage. If a nurse simply obeys the instruction and a disaster occurs, then that nurse is equally responsible. If a nurse is convinced that a doctor has made a mistake, that nurse should refuse to be involved and report to the superior nursing officer.

One area where conflict has arisen is with midwives. Different philosophies on the delivery of babies and attitudes towards the preferences of mothers have at times created tensions between home and hospital delivery options. Patient choice must be central, but doctors have the right to make their uneases known and to refuse to act in the home delivery setting. They continue to be responsible for the overall care of the pregnant woman and must be ready to act in an emergency.

Alternative medicine

Vast numbers of alternative, complementary medicines and practitioners have mushroomed from nowhere. Their success has been related to patient demand and a disillusionment with clinical medicine as it is often practised. We as patients have a right to make such choices. Doctors have an equal right and a responsibility to be sceptical about such treatments unless they can be shown to have a valid basis and successful results. Some doctors are so convinced that they are willing to refer their patients to appropriate alternative therapists. Such doctors must ensure that the patient is protected and that the therapist is genuinely qualified and competent to carry out such treatment. The doctor should also be sure that the therapy is in the best interests of the patient. These issues should be thoroughly discussed with the patient. The focus of concern on the part of doctors has been the extent to which such practitioners are properly controlled and regulated. For there to be general acceptance of such practitioners, they must be registered with and regulated by a recognised authority which has some disciplinary power to maintain standards and to safeguard patients. Providing medical information to others needs to be done only with the consent of the patient and with the assurance that such information will be used for the benefit of the patient.

Social workers are often in contact with doctors in cases of abuse of children or the elderly as they are advised to do by the Children Act 1989 and the Community Care Act 1990. The responsibility of social workers is not only for patients or clients, but also to the authority which employs them. Doctors fear that confidential information shared with a social worker might be given to a local authority to the detriment of the patient and the family. Doctors are aware of such problems and in case conferences may well give written information to the chairman alone or ask for a private hearing. Any information about patients which is shared should only be what is necessary, relevant and in the individual's or the public's interest.

Doctors and Patients

Patients involved in a practice are not just individuals, they can be seen and operate as a group. There is a growing number of patient groups being formed connected with practices and hospitals. Their aim is often to raise money for the benefit of the practice. It may also be to encourage individuals to take more responsibility for their own health by Well Woman Clinics, regular check-ups and simple disease prevention. In fund-raising, there must be no pressure on patients to contribute and no sense in which such funds may be used by doctors for items which are already paid for from other funds. Doctors must be scrupulous to ensure that any money raised is genuinely for the benefit of patients by purchasing things which would not otherwise be available.

Drug companies employ a wide variety of means to encourage doctors to use their particular products. Holidays, conferences and a whole host of 'freebies', ranging from meals to diaries and pens, are offered to doctors as an incentive to consider using a product and testing it. Patients must be assured that doctors will only recommend treatment which is appropriate, justified and which is in no way affected by any other interest the doctor may have. Doctors must not compromise themselves and their partnership with patients. The GMC has guidelines on what levels of gift are appropriate.[4] Drug companies do contribute a great deal to the advance of medicine, and major research work is funded through such companies. Patients need to know that these companies are in the business of making a profit. When they are involved in treatments or research then patients must be fully informed. Doctors are medical professionals and their clinical judgement must not be affected or seem to be so affected by financial issues and pressures.

In conclusion, doctors live and move in a network of relationships, some of which may have a great impact on the care of and relationship with patients. As patients we need to know about these relationships and the possible benefits and risks involved or any influences on the doctor and possible harm to us. Open and honest information is the way to ensure that no questions are raised about the integrity of such wider relationships. The partnership between patients and doctors depends on that honesty and the certainty that doctors are always conscious of their responsibility for the welfare and well-being of patients. They must always act in our best interests as patients and that must hold

true in all other settings and relationships where we as patients
might be harmed or disadvantaged.

Notes to Chapter 9
1. 'The Occupational Physician', *British Medical Association* booklet; *see also*
'Discipline Practice and Procedures in Employment', Code of Practice of
the Advisory, Conciliation and Arbitration Service.
2. 'Medicine Betrayed', *British Medical Journal* (1990).
3. The case of Mr Pink who was a nurse and reported dangerous staff
levels illustrates the problems for 'whistle-blowers'.
4. Department of Health Note (HN9 (62)21); Prevention of Corruption
Acts, 1906, 1916.

10

RESEARCH

It was not uncommon in the past for doctors to be 'economical with the truth'. It was unusual for doctors to discuss what they did not know and to be honest about the extent of uncertainty which is part and parcel of medicine. The growth and the success of medical knowledge has been the result not only of human creativity and intelligence, but also of failures and mistakes. We patients cannot expect doctors not to make mistakes. We can expect doctors to learn from their mistakes and not simply to bury them, in either sense of that word. When doctors were not frank with us about the limits of their own knowledge and of what medical science was able to do, it was not out of some selfish motive. Rather the aim was not to affect patient morale. To keep alive a sense of hope doctors were sometimes too positive and over optimistic. It was for our good as patients and in our best interests. To worry us with information about the dangers and uncertainties of medicine was considered to be cruel and might hinder prospects of recovery. Sometimes this has led to a great deal of anger on the part of some patients and their families. They can feel cheated when the good things they think they were promised do not happen. It is more than time for doctors and patients to be realistic about what medicine can and cannot do. Such truth and honesty lies at the core of the doctor–patient partnership.

The Individual Patient Must Come First

This is not simply a question of truth-telling. For the truth to be told, the truth must be known. This is where the importance of research is obvious. We shall see in more detail later in this chapter why research is needed, but in brief it is because there are treatments and medicines which may or may not be working well and even doing serious harm. There are new developments in treatment options, technologies and drug therapies which must be properly assessed before they are widely distributed. Doctors are scientists and their medical judgements must be based on evidence. Research plays a vital role in providing that evidence and in testing theories, claims and treatments. Medical research extends the frontiers of human knowledge and when that happens there is a clear benefit for patients. The problem is that such a benefit must not be gained at the cost of abusing patients' rights and autonomy.

While the lessons learned from research may be in our best interests as patients, we have other best interests too. Our autonomy, consent, confidentiality and integrity are equally important. In research, these moral values and dimensions must be protected, as must be the scientific accuracy and reliability of what is being tested. The aim of much of medical research is to discover the validity and effectiveness of different drugs and treatments. This must benefit us all, both as individuals and as a society. If I am ill and a new treatment is being tested on me then it may work well. I will be helped and society will gain as that valid treatment becomes a regular and normal response to that particular illness.

Research can have a bad press. Society may form pictures of mad scientists producing monsters. Frankenstein rules OK! Neither science in general, nor medical science in particular, is remotely like this. This is not because scientists are model citizens and saints any more or less than the rest of us. It is because research is carefully monitored and regulated. As medical technology has grown and enabled medicine to do remarkable and even frightening things, research in areas of life where the very fabric of society is at stake has been controlled by law.

In the case of fertility and embryo research we have seen after the Warnock Report not just new laws, but new regulatory bodies whose tasks include checking on the research that is done, issuing licences for research and ensuring that high standards are maintained. Such regulation rests on moral and legal concerns about what might happen if research was allowed to do anything and everything. There are moves to extend this kind of regulation to genetic research. The fact of the matter is that society does not believe that any group is really able to monitor and control what it does, so that justice is done and society safeguarded, and the rest of us actually see that justice and have confidence in the profession. The example of professional groups like the police, journalists and social workers monitoring their own work and mistakes hardly fills the public with confidence. Doctors need to note that if they do not keep their own house in order then society will introduce even greater restrictions on what is permitted and restrained.

Monitoring Medical Research

Medical research is controlled in three main ways. Firstly, the medical and scientific community provides a peer group review, and through journals and conferences research results are made public, tested and checked, and then become part of the medical community or are rejected. That public debate and critique is part of all scientific assessment. Unless the whole of an academic community is convinced that a new theory, treatment or procedure is valid, then it will remain unacceptable and unused. Fraud occurs in medicine as well as in every other area of life. Doctors have a scientific and moral responsibility to protect the public and the reputation of medical science by ensuring that fraud is detected and controlled. This may require some kind of national and legally founded body. Few patients will be able to function and participate in such scientific debates. Reading medical journals is pretty boring stuff unless you are part of the medical world and understand the jargon, the style, the content, the assumptions and the significance of what is being argued and debated. Secondly, the law of the land provides a safeguard for us as patients and our interests. No medical researcher can break the law with immunity. A third strand in controlling medical research is by the work of Local Research Ethics Committees. The voice and views of patients is vital to the proper functioning of both these control mechanisms.

The Law

Experimentation and research on animals have been more closely supervised than those affecting human beings. The Committee for the Safety of Drugs has regulated what may happen to humans in drug testing and research. As a result of the Warnock Report, new controls were enshrined in law to oversee research on human embryos. The Medical Royal Colleges, the British Medical Association and the General Medical Council all exercise professional guidance and control over research, but that needs to be firmly based in law and applied at a national level. International codes are common, but have no legislative power, according to the World Medical Association's Declaration of Helsinki 1964. Increasing integration into Europe may see tighter controls than exist presently. If medical research does not set its own house in order, then society will impose restrictions on research which many medical scientists will find very hard to accept. The work of Local Research Ethics Committees is now the major basis for control of research in medical centres.

Local Research Ethics Committees

The LRECs' task is to regulate medical research in hospital settings. Their membership covers doctors, nurses and patient representatives. They are increasingly being trained and the whole process of how they operate is being modified and improved. In a very real sense LRECs are the patients' watchdog. Their job is to evaluate the risks and benefits of any particular research project, not simply in medical and scientific terms but also in ensuring that the integrity, autonomy, confidentiality and rights of patients are properly protected. One of the LRECs' key tasks will be to assess the extent to which any proposed research fulfils the general aims of research. They will want to know what the likely benefit to patients will be, how treatments and drugs will be tested, and what will be learned about the development and spread of diseases. LRECs will also be concerned about the financial aspects of research. They will want to know how much it will cost, who will be paying for it, how the money will be controlled, and whether it will lead to financial gain for the researcher and/or produce more money for research. They will also recognise that publishing research results is very important for career development and progression. That in itself cannot and ought not to be avoided. There is, however, a danger that some research might simply be for career motives and that would be immoral and rejected by the LRECs.

The BMA have long argued that local committees cannot do this kind of work without having some national forum to set guidelines. There are general issues which need a high level of expertise which may only be found at the national level. Likewise the BMA is enthusiastic to ensure that there is a minimum level of legislation for the regulation and control of research. This would protect not just the patients and public, but also the researchers themselves. Some such national body would also ensure that research work and projects were not being duplicated. Where there is total independence of research work there may be no knowledge of similar work and this is a waste of money, resources and time.

Where there is any variation from standard procedures in medical treatment or any degree of actual or possible risk to patients, research must be carefully monitored. It is because there have been some unfortunate examples of the bad effects of poorly controlled and conducted research that such controls are all the more important.[1]

The Nature of Research

Research work covers a wide variety of activities. It may be an investigation of how HIV infection is spreading through the heterosexual population in the UK or whether a machine which stops snoring has side-effects or can be modified, and what impact that will have on the patient. As in all scientific research the proving of a thesis or hypothesis about an aspect of medicine requires testability and repeatability. There is something wrong with scientific results which cannot be repeated. The critical evaluation of a research project and its results by other experts is part of the nature of research. Peer review is its essence.

There are different kinds of research projects. Some will have very direct benefits for patients and are designed from the very start to test treatments which are directly relevant to patient needs, diagnoses and preferences. This will include both the modification and adaptation of existing treatments and procedures as well as testing new ones. New treatments can create their own particular moral dilemmas. The creation of a research programme in Birmingham for the use of fetal tissue which is removed and then placed in the brains of patients suffering from Parkinson's disease caused a great deal of public and professional debate. This is not the place to analyse the morality of the use of fetuses, who gives consent and what limits should be placed on such novel experiments. The point is that some kind of controls were needed and only after a LREC had examined the proposal in detail was permission given for it to proceed. In the same kind of way, work is currently being done in Exeter, where people who are dying are put on life-support machines with their own consent or that of their families. The aim is to keep their organs in good shape for transplantation when they do die.

The moral issues of using people as a means of helping others and farming organs by treating someone in intensive care, not for their own benefit but for the sake of someone else, are matched by the practical problems of what a doctor does if the patient gets better from such intensive care and what happens if an emergency patient comes in to the Intensive Therapy Unit (ITU) who really does need the bed and will die without it. Is the dying patient removed for the sake of the new patient, even though such removal will mean that fewer organs are available for transplant? Such new developments must be carefully monitored and controlled, if they are to be permitted at all. Obviously such work can create risks for the patients involved and they need to know about those risks.

There must be some doubt or uncertainty about the validity of a treatment before it becomes the basis of a research project. If there is no doubt or unknown element, it is hard to see that there should be any research project at all. Likewise, if there is no risk in current treatments and only benefits, it is hard to justify putting patients at risk by some research into a new and untested area. Such research can produce not just knowledge but new treatment and standards in treatment. When Doctor Lorber was working in Sheffield with neonates with severe abnormality, he began to codify his experience. He was then able to produce a set of criteria, giving guidelines in deciding whether or not to begin treatment which might have little or no benefit to the child, and involve a great deal of distress to child and parents, with no real prospect of reasonable quality of life.[2]

There is another broad section of research work which is purely scientific in its aim and work. There is no direct benefit to any patient. Such research is done simply to extend human knowledge. This is often called 'pure research', and conforms to the usual pattern of forming and testing a hypothesis and then seeking to disprove it in order to confirm it. Here is a classic case of using doubt to create certainty. That certainty is sustained by repeatability of results, which then issues in new laws and generally accepted procedures. It might lead to a long-term benefit for future patients, but it is more part of the basic human will and desire to understand and to know more. The remarkable thing about such research is that very often it does produce an unlooked for and unexpected benefit. Like much of science, there often seems to be an element of serendipity involved, where work in one area with one aim leads accidentally to a breakthrough in another area and direct benefit for patients. Such 'good luck' cannot be predicted or built into any research project.

Randomisation and Double-Blind Trials

In the past, when a woman discovered that she had breast cancer, then the kind of treatment she was given depended on which doctor she saw. Surgeons suggested that the best treatment for breast cancer was either a mastectomy or lumpectomy. Different surgeons disagreed about which of those was better and again a woman might have been assured by one that she needed to lose the whole of a breast, while a different doctor might only have performed the removal of a part of the breast, faced with exactly the same condition and woman. Radiologists would have argued that radiotherapy treatment was certainly the best treatment available. Those doctors who specialise in chemotherapy would have been equally adamant that their treatment was the best option. It does not take a genius to realise that all three or four treatments cannot be the best. The problem was medical bias and the preferences that particular doctors had for treatments they regarded as tried and tested. In fact, some treatments may have had little or no scientific validity. This problem was further exacerbated by the developments of new treatments and drugs, the effectiveness of which no one could be certain. To overcome medical bias and uncertainty, the randomised trial was introduced.

In part, it is a recognition of the 'witchdoctor effect'. When a doctor gives a patient a sugar pill and assures them that if they take this three times a day it will make them better, it sometimes does. The psychological role of the doctor in treatment has long been recognised and appreciated. It works to the benefit of patients. It can also work against patients. They might be given drugs which are harmful or ineffective. There might be no way of discovering the risks and damage done until it is too late.

The work of Archie Cochrane, in particular as a result of his wartime experiences, led to a general awareness that some more scientific, objective and accurate basis was required for medical treatment. Thus the randomised trial was introduced. It works on the principle of tossing a coin. When a patient presents with a problem and there is no one clear treatment but rather a set of options, then a central system randomises the patient. Each patient is then given a treatment not because it is the best one but because none of us knows which is best. Sometimes testing this treatment might include giving a placebo. That is a treatment or drug which has no active role but appears to be a genuine medicine. Such a move helps determine whether it is really the medicine which is making people better or the psychological state of the patient and the impact of the doctor. Because doctors themselves can influence what is happening in that setting, then there may be a double-blind trial. That means that neither the patient nor the doctor knows which is a genuine treatment and which is not. In dealing with drugs, many argue that this is the only way to prevent bias by the doctor and to guarantee the effectiveness of the drug. This raises a whole host of moral issues and dilemmas.

Moral issues

From the scientific point of view, such random, double-blind testing is obviously the only way to arrive at certainty. It is clearly in the best interests of all patients in the end, for it means that bad and ineffective treatment will be identified and discontinued. Others argue that in the meantime many patients will be harmed by not having treatment at all. The response to this is that patients may be affected, but that in the interests of the greatest number a few may have to suffer. They might suffer anyway in being given ineffective treatment. At least the randomised trial will lead to far greater scientific and medical certainty in the end. It is also argued that such risks are acceptable if patients know about them.

Randomised trials must only happen where there is a genuine lack of medical certainty about treatment options. If a doctor knows that a treatment is inappropriate or best for a patient then it would be wrong to give or withhold that treatment from the patient. If there is clear and accurate scientific evidence in favour of one treatment rather than another, then it is wrong to withhold that treatment from a needy patient. It is only when doctors are genuinely indifferent to different treatments and have no real preference for one treatment option over another that random trials are appropriate. Some doubt that doctors are ever really in that position. In fact, scientific research does often show that the effectiveness of a treatment is much lower than is believed, and so doctors may come to doubt what they have been doing and see the need for further research and an adequate scientific base.

Questions of consent

The major ethical problems arise with the lack of proper consent and choice on the part of the patient. There is no room for consideration of patient preferences and other values which might be at work in a patient's decision-making process. By the very nature of the trial the patient cannot know that he or she is being given a placebo or false treatment. This seems to undermine the principles of patient autonomy and choice. It would do so if we as patients did not know that we were taking part in a randomised trial. It would be totally wrong to put us into such a trial without our consent, but if the nature, risks and purpose of a randomised trial are explained then many patients may gladly give their consent to help all patients and doctors. It is claimed that when a patient realises that medicine has limits, then the patient will not lose confidence, but have more confidence because of the honesty of doctors. It is hard to see that fully informed consent is possible in such trials, for there is a lack of information and an intention and need to keep some information from the patient and the doctor. This is part and parcel of the double-blind trial, to prevent any subjective bias. It does mean that the patient does not and cannot know which treatment is being given and therefore what risks are likely. All the patient knows are the medical reasons for the trial and that there is a certain percentage chance that he or she is being given the placebo.

One of the problems with the current emphasis on patient consent is that for consent to be genuine, we as patients must be free to opt out of trials. If we decide to opt out or opt in, then we are self-selecting and in that sense it is not a genuinely random trial at all. If that is true then there can be no moral justification for the whole process. While this is a clever argument, there is considerable doubt about whether the opting in or out is itself a major factor in creating bias. Given a real randomisation process, most subjective response is controlled. Some claim that there may be undue pressure on patients to take part. This is not simply the usual kind of pressure from doctors, but that there may be no other way of receiving the particular treatment.

An example occurred in the early days of testing AZT on patients with AIDS. Knowing that there was nothing else that modern medicine could offer, many patients were desperate and willing to go to any lengths to find a cure for AIDS. It is extremely difficult to see how these patients were in a position to give or withhold genuine consent. This puts all the more onus on researchers to ensure that we as patients are properly free to opt in or out of a trial, and that our treatment is in no way conditional on the trial. Patients must be free to withdraw at any time, even though this will obviously affect the trial. As patients we must be in control of what is happening to us in research.

Fully Informed Valid Consent

In the partnership between doctor and patient a key element is trust. That trust is reinforced by the patient's awareness of the duty of the doctor to seek fully informed valid consent. The shift in this direction has been part of a civil rights and cultural shift towards the rights of the individual. It has been reinforced by a consumer-based emphasis, where the consumer controls what is happening, and this is as true in the services provided by doctors. Rather than simply replacing medical tyranny with patient tyranny, the proper way forward is in partnership. Public confidence in doctors will depend on trust in their medical skills and their personal and professional morality. We as patients need to be assured that doctors will not allow us to be put at risk in research settings from anything that will harm, damage or disadvantage us. But patients are also adults and do need to know where there are limits to medical science, or uncertainties, and where there is no known cure or accepted treatment for a disease. Many of us will gladly help where help is needed and take part in trials if this may be to our advantage. Patients must only do this based on free and genuine personal choices. Our own value systems and beliefs may encourage us to be willing to sacrifice our own health for the sake and benefit of others. We should thus be free to take part in research work which may have a degree of risk involved, as long as we fully understand what we are doing and the likely risks attached. The sad history of the rise of Nazism shows that medical science can be perverted by racist and extremist philosophies. To prevent such misuse of science and abuse and destruction of people, science must be properly and publicly controlled. That control begins with consent.

In general terms a doctor and researcher must be sure that the patient has the capacity and ability to provide valid consent. Patients must be free to make an appropriate choice and not subject to force, fraud, coercion, duress or constraint.[3] We must have sufficient knowledge and understanding to make a choice. An appropriate choice is normally defined as what a reasonable person would choose if they were in a similar situation and faced with the same facts and decision.

Choice depends on knowing what the alternatives are and their advantages and disadvantages. In new treatments this will involve being told the shortcomings of the existing and conventional treatments. The more risky the procedure involved and the more invasive the technique in question, the more emphasis there must be on the patient's grasp of all that is involved in consent. Such consent should be written and that fact recorded in the patient's medical notes and record. Consent forms can lead to abuse, where they are not accompanied by a careful discussion and plenty of opportunity for questions from the patient. Consent forms are evidence of a process and not a substitute for the process itself. Any attempt to omit consent would need exceptional justification and particularly hard cases will be discussed below.

Information

It was feared that giving patients realistic accounts of the limits of medical knowledge and science would cause panic and remove their trust in medical science. In fact, patients have welcomed the increasing honesty in doctors and the relationship as partners. Patients must be given information about the nature of the research project, why it is needed, what methods will be used, what means employed to reach conclusions, what inconveniences and hazards may be involved, what the likely impact will be in health and pain terms, and what benefits are foreseen and hoped for. In other words, before agreeing to take part in any research project, patients need to know the details and risks. As patients we also need to be assured that there is a reasonable and realistic chance of success, and told of what alternatives we might choose if we do not consent to the clinical trial.

In the USA, all possible risks of treatments and trials must be given. This is perhaps more as a protection for the researcher than for the patient. The immediate rush to law means that being sued is a very real danger for researchers and doctors. It is impossible to imagine that a patient can have all the information. The researcher may not know it all and the patient might not understand it all even if it were all on display. The standard for clinical trials and research in the UK has been to make sure that patients are adequately informed. Each individual patient may require a different process. Those responsible for explanations must recognise that the complexity of the procedures involved may not be easy to explain. There may be limitations in the ability of the patient to understand what is explained as well as the capacity of the researcher to explain what may be involved. The alternatives, including having no treatment at all, must be explained in terms of their own particular advantages and disadvantages. It is impossible to be absolutely certain about the degree of risk in any part of medicine, but that does not mean that there is no general agreement about what is likely. What most doctors would accept and what common sense dictates seem to be the usual criteria at work. Acceptable levels of explanation and of risk are what most prudent people would be happy with.

Written material can help in some cases. Such material should be expressed in a simple and straightforward way. It must contain not only details of what is involved but of the other elements in the choice and stress that the patient is free to withdraw from the research project at any time. The financial elements should not be avoided, especially if the research will lead to monetary gain for the researcher or for the hospital involved. Any written material must be used along with face-to-face discussion. It is vital that as patients we are free and able to ask any questions we wish. We may need help in formulating those questions.

Voluntary Consent

Some would doubt that any patient is ever really in a position to give free consent. The very nature of the contact between doctors and patients militates against such freedom. The desire to please the doctor is very deep in patients. When we are in hospital, dependent on the doctors for our care and getting better, it is hard for us to refuse. Doctors must be sensitive to all such pressures and try to ensure that there is no intended or unintended pressurising. As patients we can be made to feel guilty if we refuse, especially if it is a doctor who has made us much better. We can also feel selfish and unconcerned about the welfare of others. Doctors must not use emotional blackmail to persuade patients into trials. The presence of a third party at the discussion about entering a trial would be a helpful way of protecting patient autonomy. It might well be a nurse who acts with the patient as an advocate to ask the questions which are necessary and to speak up on behalf of the patient. The same problems can arise for medical students and staff involved in the research project. They too can find themselves under pressure to take part and it can be hard for them to refuse. The armed forces personnel and prison populations are particularly at risk because of the structures of authority involved. Care must be exercised in all such settings to gain genuinely valid consent. One original standard used by researchers was whether or not they would be willing to do this to themselves. It seems that researchers might be willing to do the most horrendous things to themselves for the sake of proving their own pet theories. Science has come a long way beyond this and now we as patients are seen as partners in research and so privy to all the information and help we need in our decisions about participation.

Confidentiality

This was explored in detail in the Chapter on Choice and Confidentiality, but there are particular issues which arise in research work. If there is no prospect of individuals being identified from the written or visual material in research then there is no real problem over confidentiality. Whenever and wherever there is the possibility of identification then the patient involved must both be aware of that likelihood and give consent to that information being kept and used. There must be some limits to such demands for consent if the general work of medical research is to continue. Epidemiology seeks to chart the development of diseases and their spread in the population at large. It would be impractical to seek informed consent from every single patient involved. What is possible and increasingly the case is that hospitals and teaching settings display notices and note in all their publicity literature that teaching and research is being done. As patients we are warned that this is the case and it is made clear that we may be part of such large-scale research where we will not be individually identified. If a patient wishes not to be involved then it is clear that he or she may refuse or withdraw at any point. There will be no difference in the treatment received.

When information about dead people is needed researchers must be sensitive in making any approach to relatives. With all research material the doctor remains responsible for its safety, storage and use. When a patient is being treated by someone else, then it is important that the patient tell that person or give permission for the researcher to inform the other doctor about the research project. Patients must be protected from a dual treatment setting where one might act against the other.

Ownership and Secrecy

The question may arise as to who owns the results of research work. We all like to know the end of a story and as patients who have been involved over a long period in a research project we have the right to know the results. We also have the right to know the role of any sponsor in the research and what will happen with the research material. One large sweet manufacturer agreed to fund some researching into eating sweets. It was extremely likely that the results might well not be positive towards sweet consumption. While the sponsor might prefer such information and evidence to be suppressed, the researchers were very careful indeed to make sure that they were genuinely free from bias and that their results would be published regardless of the implications for the company which paid for the work.

Who takes part in research?

We make jokes about an army sergeant asking his men for three volunteers and then pointing to three saying, 'You, you and you'. The word 'volunteer' implies a free choice. Healthy volunteers are those who are not suffering from any disease which is relevant to the research in hand. Healthy volunteers may be at risk. Even if they accept that risk, it must be clear that their interests are safeguarded. The selection, consent and conduct of the research project must protect all those involved. When something does go wrong, there must be clear lines of responsibility and a protocol for seeking compensation. Students and staff in research units are more likely to take part in trials than the rest of the population. There must be no pressure on them to participate and they must be genuine volunteers. Healthy volunteers are important in research work because they provide a view of what is normal and how healthy people react to treatments. This allows a clearer understanding of variation and departure from the norm, when sick people are involved and the results compared. Such voluntary participation also avoids the problems of coercion and of not treating those who need a treatment in order to establish the effectiveness of that treatment. But it is totally wrong to give dangerous drugs or treatments to the healthy. Where there is risk, research should be confined to those who require such treatment and not those for whom it is unnecessary. Issues of payment can create problems, for that could lead to the financially desperate volunteering all the time for any and every kind of research. Such financial incentives must be strictly controlled and monitored. All kinds of problems arise if someone does not complete the project and withdraws. Questions of payment could make a difference to the freedom to withdraw which all patients, healthy or otherwise, must enjoy.

For there to be compensation when something does go wrong in research or medicine, then negligence on the part of a researcher or medical person must be established. This does not cover sheer bad luck or accidental problems which arise unexpectedly. This could be covered if the Government introduced the idea of 'no fault compensation', where society would accept responsibility on a fixed basis when situations go wrong. This would cover cases where no one in particular is to blame yet the effects are devastating for the person injured and help would be provided.

Using Vulnerable People in Research

All of us may be dependent on doctors in hospital settings and may be judged to be vulnerable just by being there. One difficult area for ethics committees is when to allow research, if at all, that involves children, the elderly or people with mental illness or learning difficulties. If a research project could be done on people who are themselves able to give consent then there is no justification for using the vulnerable. Some would say that there should never be any research project using vulnerable people. That would be to deprive such people of the benefits of new and improved treatments and procedures. If there is no threat to the interests of the patient, little risk and some likely benefit, doctors feel that such patients can and should be involved in research. The trend in the rest of Europe seems to be stricter than in the UK, for the standards there require that there is some direct benefit for the individual.[4]

In the case of children, no one can give consent to any procedure which is not in the best interests of a child. Doctors must act to benefit the child and avoid doing harm. If a child is competent then he or she can give consent to take part in research which might give them a direct benefit. Parents should be thoroughly involved in any discussions. In the case of those whose mental capacity is affected, the degree to which different people are able to give consent varies enormously. They may well be able to give genuinely valid consent after careful and complete explanation. They are also free to withdraw and reject any participation in research. The simple rule is to gain consent if that is at all possible. Unless there is a clear benefit or absolutely minimal risk then research ought not to be conducted on such vulnerable groups. With the mentally handicapped, mentally ill and elderly, ethics committees must take particular care to safeguard those at risk.

Guidelines for the Approval and Monitoring of Research

The responsibility for the approval and monitoring of research has increasingly fallen on Local Research Ethics Committees (LRECs). Grave doubts about the composition, structure, functioning and general efficiency and competency of such committees have been expressed and shown to be a problem. The dominant role of hospital doctors and the lack of women, lay people, nurses, GPs, psychiatrists and pharmacologists were typical concerns. See the report of the King's Fund Institute on LRECs, 'Ethics and Health Care: the Role of Research Ethics Committees in the UK', 1992. The members of such committees need to be enabled to do their work by training and supervision. This still needs to be improved and extended. The BMA proposal for a national committee encapsulates one solution to a particular problem of control and monitoring. Much research now uses many different centres. It is vital for the validity of the work that all the centres follow the same protocol. If local committees disagree with some aspect and insist on such a change, then the whole project can be harmed. A national body would be in a better position to permit, control and monitor such a national level of project. An example of how such a committee might work is seen in the work of the Human Fertilisation and Embryology Authority. It is legally appointed and required to monitor research facilities and projects in embryos. The details of such work have already been indicated in the Chapter on Fertility Issues. The same process is currently in train for genetic research though the results are not yet finalised.[5]

The work of research is important for all of us. It is equally important that such research is carefully monitored and controlled. The ethical issues must be explored and the interests of all patients safeguarded. General moral rules need to be embodied in specific local, national and legally binding supervisory groups. This would ensure that doctors and patients have confidence in each other and would work together in partnership using increasingly soundly based medicine which has been shown to be valid by research.

Questions about Research

Do I understand why this research is necessary?

Do I understand what is involved if I take part in this research?

Do I understand what treatment options I may be given?

Do I understand the possible side-effects?

Do I understand the possible long- and short-term consequences of taking part?

Do I want to take part in this research?

If I do not want to take part, do I feel under pressure from the doctor to take part?

Have I expressed my worries and fears and made it clear I do not want to take part?

Am I clear what will happen to information about me given or gained during the research?

Notes to Chapter 10
1. See H.K. Beecher, 'Ethics and Clinical Research', New England Journal of Medicine 274 (1966), 1354.

2. *See* J. Lorber, 'Ethical problems in the management of myelomeningocele and hydrocephalus', *Journal of the Royal Colleges of Physicians*, Vol. 10, No. 1, October 1975.

3. *Rule* 1 of the Nuremberg Code.

4. 'Good Clinical Practice for Trials on Medicinal Products in the EC', produced by the European Commission.

5. The Department of Health Committee on the Ethics of Gene Therapy, 1989–1992, chaired by Sir C. Clothier.

11

RESOURCE ALLOCATION

It may seem odd in a book about patient choice to have a chapter on resource allocation. The history of medicine has often meant that patients have had little say or choice in how health care is distributed and how health resources are allocated. One of the main factors in the current debate is how to increase patient involvement and choice in this area. To be able to take part in the debate, we as patients need a clear grasp of how resources are allocated and to gain some flavour of how the debate is going.

Perspectives on the Problem

There will never be enough health care resources to meet all the needs and demands we as patients make. The very success of medicine in keeping people alive longer has led to more problems. Once, children and the elderly did not survive, so more money was spent on those who did survive. There have been outstanding improvements in childbirth and childcare as well as discoveries of how to keep people alive much longer. This is not just a matter of medicine. Public health improvements, a higher standard of living, better diet, housing and education have all meant that most of us live much longer than our ancestors. Because of medical improvements, more of the treatment and resources are focused on the seriously ill. We expect medical service to do more and more. The reality is that those who are intractably ill take an increasing proportion of the health care budget. As more people survive and survive longer, the greater their expectation about their quality of life and their demand from medics to meet these desires. It can appear that, with the success of medicine and the marvels of medical technology, we can discover cures for all diseases, if we spend enough money and make sure scientists work together. The fly in this ointment is the economic reality of a world recession, the battle against inflation and the spiralling cost of drugs and treatments, especially those based on new technologies. Society is driven back to try to answer hard questions about how best to meet the needs and demands of the nations as well as the world's population. What are to be the priorities and goals in health care? If the cake is going to be small, how should it be cut? We may have to ration our limited resources.

In reality, rationing decisions have always been made. How much time a doctor spends with a patient, uses to do research, or takes to fill in forms needs to be decided; it also reveals the priorities chosen. In war situations, medical personnel have been faced with overwhelming numbers of casualties. Some kind of rationing system has to be used. Generally it meant that those who were going to die anyway and those who could survive anyway were not treated. Those who would benefit from medical treatment were given the precious time and care. None of us can be very comfortable about such broad and basic categories, but it is better than pretending that we are not making choices at all.

The rationing that has been part of the NHS has not always been done openly. In a way, society has expected so much from the National Health Service. It was supposed to meet not only health care needs but to provide basic welfare for all. This was a recipe for irregularity and the way in which resources were allocated was largely decided by personalities and power struggles between competing medical specialists. With a division now between purchasing and providing health care, the need for explicit criteria is obvious.

The problem of limited resources

The experience of the problems of resource allocation in medicine in the UK has suffered from a number of confusions. Long before the current economic downturn, health professionals were discussing the moral, political and practical issues of resource allocation in health matters. As our ability to forecast the trends of health care and measure the patterns has developed, so the assessment of the success rates of various treatments has become possible. Such information allows us to make rational and well-informed choices about what treatments are best and which diseases will grow and need more resources. Economists, administrators and doctors have been working on the development of various economic models in health care. This is now seen as part of good medical practice and will increasingly become a major issue in the development of the health services.

Doctors have become involved in the political question of whether more money should be spent on health care in opposition to increased funding for education, housing or pensions. The governmental changes in the National Health Service have created pressure on doctors and health care institutions to examine the allocation of resources. Doctors must not only provide good medical care but they must also create value for money, maximise patient choice and be thoroughly efficient. If they are, then in our new market economy of health care – where money follows patients – the more successful doctors, general practices and hospitals will have more money. That inevitably means less for the others.

Such changes raise very fundamental questions about the balance between prevention, care and the treatment of disease. Should more money be spent on stopping diseases before they happen, or in caring for and curing people who have the disease? Before we consider how we might even begin to confront such a question, we need to focus on a confusing debate over medical audit.

Medical Audit

When the medical world sees the word 'audit', it divides. For the administrators and accountants 'audit' means financial assessment based on some kind of cost-benefit analysis. To many doctors such a narrow view of medicine, patients and treatment is negative, reduces patients to sums of money and numbers in the business of maximising throughput and profit. In contrast, *medical audit* for many doctors concerns what counts as good medical practice. It seeks to correct clinical mistakes. It covers science, morality, psychology, and clinical judgement and treatment, as well as financial sensitivity. For such an audit to happen doctors need solid peer group review and assessment. A medical audit involves a clear understanding of what is actually happening, judgements about the appropriateness of that and of the needs and demands made on health care and doctors. It explores ways of improving and working towards greater personal, managerial, medical, professional and financial efficiency.

The first step in good audit is to examine how effectively existing resources are being used. Treatments and drugs need to be cost-effective as well as clinically successful. Doctors are seeking not just to improve the *quantity* of health care and its delivery, but also to maintain and improve the *quality* of that care. Treating patients is not just a matter of how much it costs. It is also about the quality of the doctor–patient relationship and the care and treatment provided. Doctors are deeply uneasy about any false stress on cost and financial perspectives, especially if these begin to affect the way doctors see and relate to patients, and the way patients perceive and relate to doctors. What is now happening needs to be carefully and thoroughly assessed before we can demand more money and resources from central government.

Resource Allocation in Practice

There are two different elements in resource allocation which affect us as patients and the choices we have. The first is the development of such resources. The second is how to distribute them. Developing resources usually means creating extra funding. For some this is the answer to all the allocation problems in health care. If only the Government would give more money then we as patients would have the treatments we needed when we needed them. To persuade the Government involves aggressive political consultation and canvassing the general public to create pressure on the Government through local MPs. Another way of developing resources would mean greater stress on educating the public to take more responsibility for its own health care. There have been significant shifts in what is called 'preventive' medicine. If the problem can be solved before it becomes a medical problem and a drain on limited resources, so much the better. Campaigns against smoking and warnings against the dangers of AIDS are examples of such an educational and preventive thrust. Encouraging women to have cervical smears clearly prevents many unnecessary deaths from cervical cancer. Different strategies are used to cut down the numbers affected by diseases, which are extremely expensive for the health services as well as often fatal for the patient.

Even if we do put greater resources and effort into the prevention of disease and public health education, that in itself will not remove the difficult questions of resource allocation. At a very simple level, these decisions mean making judgements between prevention of disease or curing illness. To complicate this division, the cost of care has to be weighed. When we talk of cost we must not simply think in terms of money. If we spend on one area of care – care, prevention or cure – or on one particular treatment, then we cannot spend that money on something else. To treat one patient may be to deprive others. Doctors are faced then with some hard choices. As they make them, the 'cost' factors include time, stress on doctors and patients, and a downturn in the quality of care and the partnership between doctors and patients.

Increasing medical costs

Different kinds of ways of measuring what happens already, could form the basis for decisions about what should happen. As part of assessing and controlling the quality of care, doctors are trying to measure health outcomes. Treatments are compared to see which are the most effective. Priorities in health care are much more widely discussed between doctors and health administrators. The general public has as yet played little part in this discussion. For the debate to make sense, rational scientific standards must be formed as a proper basis for decisions. Technology and new drugs have increased not just doctors' capacity to keep people alive and treat previously so-called 'untreatable' diseases, but also the cost of medical treatment. Neonatal care, transplantation, Intensive Therapy Units (ITU), and a whole host of new diagnostic tools have all put pressure on the limited resources available. Competing demands mean hard decisions must be faced and taken.

One tool that has been developed by health economists for such decision-making is the idea of QALYS, Quality Adjusted Life Years.[1] This tried to measure the *quantity* of life in terms of the number of years which a patient might gain from a treatment, as well as the *quality* of life enjoyed by the patient. In reality it is a simple form of cost-benefit analysis. The concept was heavily criticised as being unjust, simplistic, created by those who had no direct involvement with patients and not really taking account of the wider range of moral and emotional issues at stake. If QALYS were introduced as a basis for rationing resources, then the elderly would be unlikely to be treated. Their number of life years and quality of life would be very low in comparison with fertility treatment, where because of screening and the commitment of parents to having a child, the new-born baby would have both the prospect of a high quality of life and very many years of healthy life. Even if this solution is no solution, the problem of resource allocation remains.

Who gets what care?

There can be no doubt that we need to allocate our medical and health resources more effectively. People who need treatment are either having to wait far too long before they get it, or do not even get what they require. In practice, the age of a person is used in decisions not to give such things as transplants, even if the patient needs it. Our national treatment rates do not always compare very favourably with other countries in Europe and even less favourably with the United States. The numbers who receive infertility, psychological and psychiatric and basic rehabilitation help are limited. The waiting times for orthopaedic and plastic surgery services are far too long. Governments and doctors are trying to overcome some of these problems by cutting down waiting lists. This can be done simply by removing people from the list for a while and then adding them later when someone else has been treated and created a space. Justice must not just appear to be done, but must actually be done.

In a sad way we have not moved very far beyond the situation where penicillin was first introduced and doctors had to decide who should benefit from this new and expensive drug. George Bernard Shaw presented a dilemma for a doctor. He pictured having to make a choice between two people for a life-saving treatment. One person was morally good. The other was morally bad. The problem was that the bad person was highly creative and would contribute to society. The good person would not. The doctor's dilemma was to decide between goodness and badness, or creative contribution to society and no benefit at all. What Shaw's doctor's dilemma does show is that we need clear criteria and an agreed framework for decisions about the allocation of resources. To reach or create such agreement is difficult in a pluralistic society, where there seems little moral consensus. Doctors and patients must explore together, at the local and national level, what kind of priorities we accept and how we ought to allocate limited resources.

Who decides?

Patients need to know who makes rationing decisions and what the basis of such decision-making is. Usually patients and the general public play little part in resource allocation decisions. That does not mean that the public is not concerned about these issues. When a young girl was unable to be treated in the UK because there were no adequate resources, the public raised a great deal of money to pay for treatment in the USA. The public have also raised vast amounts of money for scanner appeals, where there was no funding for such 'high-tech' equipment. Public protests and action through the media do make a difference. As actual and potential patients, especially if we suffer from particular diseases which may be under-resourced, we have a right and a responsibility to speak out, to campaign, and to urge Parliament, local health authorities and medical organisations to meet the medical needs of our society. Geriatric care, community and institutional care for the mentally disordered, and health care for the poor are all under-resourced. These groups of people are all too easily excluded from proper care and treatment.

The partnership between patients and doctors should be matched by a partnership between doctors and the Government. The Department of Health has ultimate responsibility for our health budgets and increasingly affects the treatments patients receive by the choice of priorities at central level. The Department is firmly committed to cutting down waiting for patients, both in time on lists for treatment and time in hospitals waiting to be seen and treated by a doctor. Doctors are concerned that these priorities are not accurately and properly monitored. Doctors feel that too much money is spent on administration and too little on the actual care and treatment of patients.

Doctors in general practice and in hospital Trust settings control their own budgets and are responsible for how they allocate their resources and decide on priorities. This power must be limited by a basic responsibility for patients at risk, including the very young and the very old. It is important for patients that doctors are thoroughly involved with Government decisions that affect the health and best interests of patients. Doctors do have to consider the wider implications of their decisions to treat or not to treat. There are limits to resources and doctors must consider how best to use these resources, not just for the benefit of an individual patient, but also for all patients.

Cheaper alternative drugs

A doctor has a clinical, professional and ethical duty to treat each individual patient, bearing in mind the most economic and successful treatments available. Too often doctors have fought for more money to treat their own patients and ignored the patients of other doctors. Doctors have to consider the cost of treatment and of different drugs. If there is a cheaper alternative and no significant loss in benefit, then doctors should prescribe that drug and not a more expensive one. Even if patients have heard of and ask for a named drug which is costly, doctors should encourage the use of cheaper alternatives, if these are available and equally good. To make decisions between alternative drug therapies or different treatments requires solid scientific evidence. Doctors need to do the necessary research on the results and outcomes of different treatments and drugs and have a duty to keep themselves well informed about such information. Governments have a parallel duty to make such information available. Currently, doctors receive extra payments if they attend courses designed to bring them up to date with new developments in the various areas of medicine. It is only sad that a financial incentive is needed at all.

Patient choice is a central core in the doctor–patient relationship. Decisions about the use of expensive life-preserving treatments need to be made with the patient, as well as other medical and nursing staff. Conflicts can arise between GPs and hospital doctors. For example, to treat growth disorders in young people is a costly business. The danger is that disagreements over who is responsible for the patient – the GP or the hospital – can lead to the patient not being given a necessary drug or treatment.

Doctors and patients have to recognise that there comes a point where there is little or no benefit in continuing treatment. To do so is a waste of money. Patients and doctors may then have to decide to stop or withdraw a treatment, as in dealing with a severely handicapped baby who is unlikely to survive. Basic care, comfort and tender love must never be withdrawn. Pointless medical treatments which have no real benefit and are costly cannot be demanded or expected by patients or their families. To continue futile medicine is in fact to deprive other needy patients of vital medical treatment and care.

What principles guide resource decisions?

Until recently and even now, most of us as patients remain ignorant about how resource choices are made and the criteria used to make those decisions. Rationing does happen, but it should be done openly. It should also be based on rational and scientific evidence and not just the subjective whim of a doctor or Government minister. When society does make decisions about how rationing is to be done, as many different groups as possible must be involved, especially doctors and patient bodies. All of these groups must be held responsible for the results and consequences of such decisions. Society ought not to blame doctors for decisions we all must take. There should be careful public and professional scrutiny of the criteria used and the decisions made. What then are the kind of criteria we might or already do adopt?

Treat According to Need

Traditionally, the major medical criterion for treatment has been the need of the patient. But what is need? While we can all debate the finer points of definitions, there can be no real doubt about the difference between living and dying, ordinary and extraordinary treatments, and reasonable and unreasonable needs. We all know what is essential for life and have a pretty good idea about what we need to flourish as human beings. We know what good health means in general terms. When we are confronted with different needs, then we shall try to meet the greatest and most urgent ones. Emergency needs always come first. Until and unless life is preserved, no decisions can be made about the state of the patient and what will be best for him or her. Part of an appropriate response to urgent needs is to consider the likely success of emergency treatment. If there is little or no likelihood of a successful outcome, then there is no obligation on doctors to begin or to keep on trying with that treatment.

We must distinguish carefully between what someone needs and what he or she wants. Needs and wants or desires fall into different categories. An infertile woman may want to have a baby. It is much less clear that it is a medical need. I may want a different nose line, but that is more a desire on my part than a need. Normally such areas of medical practice are elective, where individuals choose to have something done which is not strictly necessary. Doctors are under no obligation to meet all our wants. The responsibility to meet people's needs does not mean that doctors must meet a patient's every wish, demand or want. Doctors are not simply need-meeters. The good doctor must be able and willing to refuse to do what a patient wants. It might be possible to take this distinction between needs and wants further by offering a description of what human beings require as human beings in contrast to what particular individuals may want for themselves because of the kind of person they are and the experiences they have had. This might lead to a basic health care package for us all. This core would be paid for through the National Health Service. Anything above and beyond the core would have to be funded privately. Treatment which was necessary would have to be effective as well as an efficient use of resources. Such treatment would be the responsibility of society and not the individual.[2]

The commitment to need as the basis for treatment would remove one trend in society. Some of the public are critical of treating patients who have what are sometimes called 'self-inflicted' injuries. If someone smokes, goes hang-gliding, engages in irresponsible sexual behaviour, or drinks and drives and is then injured, there are those who feel that society is not obliged to treat such cases. This would be a very frightening move and have devastating results. Imagine an Accident and Emergency Unit where a patient is rushed in with severe injuries. The medical team would scramble around trying to discover if these injuries were caused because of foolish and risky behaviour on the part of the patient or were a genuine accident, rather than simply responding to need. Insurance companies may discriminate between risky professions and activities. Medicine should continue to meet genuine needs, wherever these needs can be met by doctors. Society must make adequate resources available for these needs to be met by doctors. Treatment should be according to need.

Treat According to Merit

Giving people what they deserve is a complicated business. The debate over self-inflicted injuries found a clear focus in an article by Digby Anderson in *The Sunday Times* during 1990. He wrote: 'However, what about those who elect to be promiscuous and thereby acquire sexually transmitted diseases including AIDS; who experiment with addictive drugs; who persist in lifestyles which render them likely to heart disease or cancer; who, without due preparation, climb up mountains or down potholes. They do these things for enjoyment; then, when their indulgences have unhealthy consequences, they are bailed out by the taxpayers who fund this treatment.'

It is not easy or simple to give people what they deserve. It seems that disease is much more a matter of genetic history than of the choices we make. Are we then to be treated or not because of something over which we have absolutely no control? Some jobs have to be done and are very dangerous. It seems grossly unfair to discriminate against people because of the job they do and the risks they have to run in order to do that job.

Treating according to merit or desert would mean both what individuals deserve in themselves because of who and what they are, and also what they desire because of what they have done or might do for others. It would cover both past achievement and possible future contributions. In essence, this is to judge who should be treated according to some kind of calculation of social worth. That worth would cover both what society itself deems to be worthy and the benefit actually produced for society. In practical terms it means that Nobel Prize winners are to be treated before or instead of the ordinary man in the street.

This kind of utilitarian, discriminatory, social-worth philosophy sits very uneasily with the way doctors are trained and practise medicine. Their basic attitude is not to try to measure the social standing of a patient, but rather to respond to the needs and distress of someone who is ill. Who and what that person is is irrelevant, as far as the right to treatment is concerned. It is difficult to see that society would ever be able to reach agreement about who deserves to be treated based on the criterion of social worth. The worth of a person rests in his or her own personhood, not on what is contributed to society.

Treat According to the Ability to Pay

A genuine market-place philosophy would mean that those who can afford to be treated are treated. It also means that those who cannot afford treatment, do not get treated. Few of us would be very keen to state this view publicly, but in practice any system of health insurance and private medical care schemes ends up with this situation. This may be clearly seen in what happens in that champion of free-market enterprise – the United States. Those who can afford it are not simply given treatment, but are probably over-treated. When you have paid for something, you want to make sure you get the very best and all you paid for, regardless. At the other extreme, the poor in the USA may not be treated at all. Careful scrutiny of the US health care system reveals that the worst off are not those in total poverty, for the Government does provide them with some basic health care. Instead, those who are actually the worst off are the people who are in work and do earn, but not enough to afford proper insurance or treatment. They cannot get health care and are not entitled to Government funding for treatment. The overall loss to society from those who are not treated is a serious financial issue, as well as a moral and emotional tragedy. The sheer waste of people and resources is frightening. The UK would do well to learn the sad lessons from the US and make sure that ability to pay is not the basic or sole criterion for receiving medical care and treatment.

Treat Equally

Treating patients equally means treating similar cases similarly and different cases differently. At the heart of the concept of justice

lies the notion of fairness. In health terms it must mean that there
is no bias or unwarranted discrimination. We need to be careful
what we say here. It is nonsense to suggest that doctors do not,
cannot and ought not to be discriminating. Good medicine requires
careful discussion between different cases and people. What is being demanded is moral and medical consistency, universalisability,
which means doing the same thing in the same circumstances, and
non-discrimination on false or inappropriate grounds. If a doctor
treats two similar cases differently, there must be a good medical
reason for that difference. In practice, the morality of equal treatment
reduces to equal access to treatment.

Random selection for treatment

At a conference of clergy and hospital chaplains, I invited them to
make a hard medical choice. I portrayed a situation where there was
only one kidney for transplant, and three people who needed it, or
else they would die, and that this kidney was a perfect match for all
three. One was a prostitute, another a playboy and the third person
a poet. The clergy were asked to make the choice of who should get
the kidney. Many were in favour of the prostitute. They felt that she
gave the greatest happiness to the greatest number. Others favoured
the playboy for he spent money, which created wealth and jobs for
others. Only one thought that the poet should be preserved in the
name of culture. When the final vote was taken, almost all voted
for a fourth option. They wanted to draw lots.

Random selection might seem like a good idea, for it certainly
involves equality of opportunity. The problem is that patients do not
all become ill at the same time. Doctors cannot tell how much care
and treatment each patient will need when a medical procedure is
begun. Emergencies will always intervene in such a system. Random
selection might prevent subjective and arbitrary judgements and
puts the responsibility on the system itself rather than on the person
who would have to make a choice. Who is treated and who is not
depends on luck and not on the doctor or the patient. In the end,
the real basis for treatment is 'first come, first served'. In one sense,
this can be seen as simply meeting patient needs as and when they
arise. More controversially, some will feel a system which sets strict
budgetary limits means inevitably that people who need treatment

early in the financial year will be treated. Those who arrive later in the year will find that there is not enough money left and so will get no treatment at all. This is less than fair and hardly suggests careful management of limited resources.

Treat According to the Right to Treatment

While it is tempting to argue that human beings and citizens of a particular nation have a right to be treated, it is far from clear what the basis of such rights is. There are no rights without corresponding responsibilities on the part of someone else. Law might confer rights and responsibilities on people. It is less obvious that there are such things as natural rights. World starvation and global disease where millions suffer and die seem to indicate the ineffectiveness of claiming the right to treatment, far less the right to life. The scope of such rights could be endlessly debated. The right to die and the right to live, the right to have a baby and the right to abortion on demand are good examples of the disagreement and contradictoriness of rights claims. In addition, there would be an ever escalating and never satisfiable list of health rights claims. It is not clear that talk of rights will be much help in decisions about how to allocate resources.

So what?

It is all too easy to find fault with all these criteria. Need and justice seem the most basic and fundamental principles. The history of medicine has been a history of loving service by doctors and nurses. This service has been for the benefit of others, responding to human need whenever and wherever it occurs, and tries to treat everyone fairly, appropriately and justly. We cannot escape from the problems of resource allocation and that will inevitably mean specifying what basic health needs people have and society agrees to meet. It means careful testing of the success of different treatments and drugs. It will involve setting priorities about patient care and treatment. It must certainly take account of what patients want. No one of us as patients has a totally free choice, but modern medicine is at its best and most moral when it seeks to allow patients involvement in the decisions that affect them at every level.

The way forward

In taking the debate forward there are four areas which require our attention as doctors and patients. We must work to create an agreed moral framework for decision-making and then try to set priorities for the whole of society. Resource allocation is a matter for us all and not just for health care professionals or for politicians. Patient choice is not simply about individual patients choosing what treatment they will participate in and which they will refuse. It is also patients as a whole group expressing their own sets of priorities and concerns for resource allocation. This is not to allow the public, or the politically elected, to make health resource decisions by imposition. Neither can nor ought doctors try to do the same. All of us must be invited to grapple with resource decisions, for they affect all of us and are the responsibility of us all. Collective wisdom, responsibility and resourcefulness must be pooled to create decisions with which we can live and die. The Black Report[3] showed clearly that health care and inequalities are not simply medical matters, but relate to a complex web of social, housing, employment, family and economic factors. Medicine and medical resource allocation alone will not improve the health of the nation.

Doctors and patients must work to create an agreed factual basis for rational and scientific decision-making. The sheer variety of economic models, outcome measurements and assessment criteria needs a sound, objective, scientific basis. The facts need to be clearly established and the criteria for what constitutes factual evidence agreed. Health and disease in terms of morbidity, mortality and disability must all be set out in descriptive terms which are valid and comprehensive. The scales used must be consistent. There must also be valid criteria for resource judgements, with some clear and consistent means of establishing results.

In partnership, doctors and patients must work for changes and shifts in strategies. These changes must be based on how best to fulfil the aims selected in light of the facts and priorities agreed. Inevitably this will mean more education, political activity and public debate, as well as lobbying and setting the medical houses in order, if that is necessary and appropriate. A key part of a doctor's responsibility is to treat all patients justly.

We need more and better understanding of what is involved in medical audit. That will mean a shift from the stress on the financial aspects of audit to an emphasis on good medical practice. Health care professionals have nothing to fear from increased awareness of better practice, and the knowledge that doctors are learning from their mistakes will not only promote public confidence in the profession, but will add to professional pride. This means continuing, comprehensive, soundly based and sensitively practised audit. The good doctor will not bury his or her mistakes but always be willing to learn from them in order to improve the practice of medicine.

The conclusion of this chapter is clear, issues of resource allocation will not disappear. The need for such decision-making will only grow. Patients must not leave this task to doctors alone and even less to politicians. The voice of the patient must be heard loudly and clearly.

Notes to Chapter 11

1. *See* R. Rosser, 'From health indicators to quality adjusted life years: technical and ethical issues' in A. Hopkins and D. Costain (eds.), *Measuring the outcomes of medical care* (Royal College of Physicians, London, 1990).

2. 'Choice in Health Care, a report by the government committee on choices in health care, the Netherlands, 1992' (Dunning Report).

3. D. Black, P. Townsend, and N. Davidson, 'Inequalities in Health: The Black Report', Harmondsworth, Penguin, 1982.

12

VALUES, PHILOSOPHY AND PRACTICE

Doctors are busy, practical people. Patients do not expect them to sit and think about what they are doing, but to do it. Doctors have values, beliefs and philosophies which underlie their practice. Many of those values and outlooks are personal. Others are taught and are part of what it means to belong to the medical profession. Doctors are people too, so, like the rest of us, they are often a mixture of different values. What is important for us as patients is to know the kind of values which are generally agreed among doctors.

In one sense, we are crying for the moon. We live in a multi-faith, multi-cultural, pluralistic society, where there are many competing world views and value systems. The sheer variety of moral values makes agreement and consensus difficult to achieve. Yet there is a remarkable level of agreement among doctors on moral values. As patients would disagree with each other about how these values apply to different issues, so doctors disagree and are entitled to do so. Generally speaking, the medical profession is fairly conservative on moral issues. This may be because of the special role of power that doctors exercise over patients and in society. Doctors together are a powerful force and have been very successful over the years in making their voice heard and influencing Government policy. At times, doctors' organisations function like trade unions, preserving the salaries, rights and privileges of their members. These organisations also play a wider role by giving doctors specific advice on moral and professional issues. It is to their credit that they seek the help and input of people like lawyers, the clergy and philosophers, who bring a different perspective to these issues.

Medical Codes

The history of medicine is in part a history of doctors trying to regulate themselves. Like all professional groups, they have had sets of rules which were the basic minimum or even the high ideals that doctors should have and practise. There has been a significant shift in these codes of practice. In the past, much of the context was more about how doctors should relate to each other than how they should deal with us as patients. Doctors should not say nasty things about each other. They should pay their bills on time. They should keep each other informed as they transfer patients from one to the other doctor. Now, in a society where patient choice is at the heart of medical ethics, there has been a fundamental shift of power and of what counts as important within the medical profession. Modern codes[1] of medical ethics are much more patient-oriented. What is important for patients is not so much to know the details of these codes, but to discern the values and philosophies which underlie them.

Doctors are busy people so they tend to work on a case-by-case approach. As they gain experience and practise medicine, they pick up skills as well as knowledge, not just about medicine, but also about people and how to relate to them. Many of us will be familiar with the portrait of consultants in the *Carry on, Doctor* film. It seemed as if ninety-five per cent of consultants thought they were only answerable to God and the other five per cent did not even accept that limitation. Times have changed and doctors are increasingly aware of the ethical and moral issues and the need for the profession to state where it stands and the moral basis from which it operates.

Power and Vulnerability

When we are ill, we are vulnerable. The word 'patient' comes from a Latin word which has two meanings – to suffer or to allow. Patients suffer. They also allow doctors to know a great deal of personal, private information about them, and to do things which are deeply intimate and can be embarrassing. With this kind of information and permission to do things to patients' minds and bodies, doctors have power over us. We patients need to be sure that this power will not be abused and will be properly used in our best interests.

Where there is power, there needs to be even greater responsibility than we normally expect from people. We do expect higher standards of behaviour from doctors in their dealings with patients. We do not expect doctors to take advantage of patients sexually, financially or in any way that will do harm to the patient. Doctors are expected to treat patients who have highly contagious and infectious diseases, even when the doctor might catch the disease. In this way, doctors are to be self-sacrificial. Society needs to be clear and careful about this. We do not and cannot demand that doctors are silly and throw their lives away needlessly, although society does expect doctors to act in situations where they will be at risk for the benefit of the patient.

Doctors are answerable to patients and to society at large. The General Medical Council controls doctors. Doctors must be registered with the GMC before they are allowed to practise medicine. If they behave improperly and do not do their job as doctors then they can be reported to the GMC, who may strike them off the register, suspend or reprimand them. The GMC is not only concerned with high professional standards, but also moral ones. Even if at times it appears to defend doctors and their interests, their real task is to protect patients from doctors who abuse their power over vulnerable people.

Underlying Values

We live in a country which has been largely based in Judaeo-Christian values. These values were often related to Greek philosophy and thought. It is no surprise then to discover that most medical ethics begin with the Hippocratic Oath. While Greek ideas were important, they were not the only influences on medical philosophy and practice. The Jewish and Christian faiths contain many fundamental moral values and teachings. It is interesting to note how fundamental these values still are in our society, which is secularist and post-Christian.

The Ten Commandments deal with right family and sexual relationships, the sanctity of life, truth-telling and the danger of greed and selfishness. Doctors are involved with patients, not just as individuals but as members of families and communities. Doctors are in the business of ensuring healthy bodies, minds and relationships. To practise medicine there needs to be a basic level of truth in the partnership between doctors and patients. We do not expect doctors to tell us lies. We do expect to be told, know and understand the truth about our situation, illness, treatment, options and the likely outcome. We depend on the doctor's commitment, not just to the sanctity of life in general, but to caring for and preserving our life. We do not expect doctors to become sexually involved with patients. If and when they do, such sexual activity is met with serious professional punishment. We assume that doctors are not treating us for their own financial gain, but are acting in our best interests. Obviously, doctors do and deserve to make a living from medicine. That is very different from taking financial advantage of patients, either in the use of facilities, relationships with drug companies or other doctors, or in giving unnecessary and expensive treatments. The financial responsibility of doctors covers not just a responsibility to individual patients but to society as a whole, especially in the allocation of limited resources.

The Ten Commandments give a clear expression to the underlying values which doctors accept and patients expect. Christians and Jews believe that it is not possible to fulfil the standards affecting human relationships properly without reference to God and the other five commandments. It is interesting to note how many doctors have a religious faith and the way such faith guides the practice of medicine. Many doctors have no religious faith, but still accept and live by the professional and moral standards society demands and expects. These standards have been expressed in lots of different ways, but have found their main expression in four principles put forth by Beauchamp and Childress.[2] These principles are do no harm, do good, autonomy and justice.

Do No Harm

The most basic rule in medical ethics is to do no harm (*non nocere* or non-maleficence). This is a minimum standard. It describes a defensive stance where the doctor seeks only to avoid doing harm.

The problem is that life is not all cut and dried and in treating patients doctors may have to do some harm in order to do good in the longer run. Giving patients drugs is giving them the means to harm themselves. Too much of some drugs will do us harm. Operations are painful businesses and certainly do harm to the body. However, the clear aim of giving drugs or doing operations is not to harm the patient, but to do them good.

Harm is not just a physical matter. Our reputation and standing in the community can be harmed. Careless talk costs lives and reputations. This is part of why patients' confidentiality is so important. Doctors are to avoid harming patients physically, mentally and in their relationships with other people. Unfortunately, situations do arise where doing harm to one person or group may be justified in order to avoid greater harm to others. If someone is putting the lives of others at risk because he or she is HIV positive and refuses to tell a spouse, or if someone is subject to fits and continues driving without informing the authorities, then doctors may and must protect the majority and those at risk, even if it harms the patient involved.

In the Chapters on Research and Suicide and Euthanasia, the need for doctors to avoid harm was stressed. However, these situations may involve patients who are willing to be harmed for the benefit of others. Medical morality deals with this by making sure that people know what they are doing and the risks and harm involved. In research, people may agree to painful tests and procedures which will do them harm, but will lead, hopefully, to long-term benefit at least for others. There are limits to how much harm doctors may inflict on people, even if they are willing. In the Cox case[3], where a doctor gave a lethal injection to a patient who was in extreme pain, the defence agreed that the patient, as well as her family, wanted her to die. In law, it makes no difference that a patient is willing to be harmed. If a child can in any sense be 'happy' to be aborted, or a wife 'happy' to be 'beaten up', or masochists 'happy' to be injured, that in no way justifies the doing of harm. Killing people is an extreme form of doing harm and doctors are morally and legally forbidden to commit euthanasia.

Do Good

Doing good, being beneficent, or acting in people's best interests is the positive and other side of avoiding harming people. Doing no harm is minimised and ultimately self-protective. Doing good is a positive thing and involves taking initiatives to benefit other people. It calls for greater effort on the part of the doctor. The motive for such doing of good is usually compassion. It is because we sympathise with and feel love and concern for others, that we try to act in their best interests. Doctors cannot be expected to like all their patients. They can be expected to act compassionately and in the patient's best interests, because the patient is ill, vulnerable and in a partnership relationship with the doctor. Doing good is a response to need, and patients need doctors, their skills and advice, and their genuine concern for them.

Acting in the best interests of patients can lead to paternalism. To do his or her best for a patient, the doctor must know what is best. The danger then is that in knowing and seeking to do what is best the doctor may interfere with a patient's free choice and decision. When it comes to doing good, then, doctors are not just dealing with treatments. They are also trying to do good to and for the person. That means encouraging and allowing the person to make his or her own decisions and to take increasing responsibility for himself or herself. The doctor is to help us in that process and to be sensitive to the times when it is too hard for us to decide or cope with such decisions. Then the doctor should accept the load we want to put on medical shoulders, but that load should only be passed over for a while. The doctor's aim must be to enable each patient to take as much responsibility as possible. This is for the patient's benefit and is a vital part of doing good. This is what respect for us as patients involves and is often called autonomy.

Autonomy

Patient choice is the central focus of autonomy. Respect for each of us as individuals means that we are to be given as much choice and control over what happens to us as possible. The excepted situations, where we are not able to exercise that choice, do not affect the fundamental and normal stress on the freedom of us as patients to make decisions for ourselves. Doctors are not allowed to force their wishes on us. Even if the doctor does know best, we patients must be free to do what we want with our own bodies and to have both our bodies and our wishes respected. Privacy, consent, confidentiality and choice are the expressions of autonomy. Doctors have a responsibility to maximise patient involvement in their treatment and to encourage and enable us to make fully informed, valid decisions about what happens to our own bodies.

Autonomy is never an absolute in society. Our rights and freedoms are always restricted, usually on two particular grounds. We are not free to interfere with the rights, freedom and autonomy of other people. If we put others at risk, then society and doctors have a duty to protect those at risk. That may mean limiting the autonomy and freedom of a patient in the interests of others. The second limitation comes from a concern to minimise harm to the patient himself or herself. If it is in the best interests of a patient, then his or her autonomy can be limited or removed. Both of these grounds are very serious steps to take and involve hard decisions for doctors about the public good and the individual's best interests. The doctor is not allowed to force his or her own values on a patient. Doctors must make the very best clinical judgement they can, then act on that basis and be able and willing to justify the limiting of a patient's rights and freedoms when called in question by the patient, his representative or the law.

The law itself is the clearest expression of the rights of patients and the duties of doctors. There are no rights without corresponding responsibilities. If patients do have rights, then usually it is the job and responsibility of the doctor to safeguard those rights. To act otherwise is a breach of the professional and ethical standards of medicine. It is also unjust.

Justice

The fourth principle at the heart of medical ethics is justice. There are many different accounts and definitions offered, but the essential core is treating patients fairly, making sure that similar cases are dealt with in the same way, and different cases individually. Some might interpret this as a call for equality.

Often justice is embodied in the laws of a land. Doctors, like all of us, are subject to these laws and will be punished if they break the law. Justice seeks to go beyond the mere letter of the law in ensuring equal treatment for people and no wrong kind of discrimination against individuals or groups. The area where justice is most hotly debated in current medical thinking is the allocation of resources. Given that the amount of money we have is limited and the demands made by patients endless, how are these limited re-sources to be allocated? In the chapter devoted to this theme, we offered a number of ways of defining just ways of distributing resources. Doctors must be involved in these hard decisions, for their clinical experience and judgement is vital if such choices are to have any rational and scientific basis.

At the very practical level, justice will mean for doctors that they do not act unfairly towards patients. In the position of power doctors are entrusted with, the abuse of power and people can happen. As patients we are entitled to justice from doctors. We should be dealt with not just according to the law of the land, but also fairly and equitably by doctors. We should not be discriminated against on improper and unjust grounds. Our rights and freedoms should be protected. Doctors act justly when they treat patients properly as people and as needing medical help in their vulnerability.

How Doctors Learn and Practise Medicine

Doctoring and medicine cannot be learned from books alone. Of course, it is possible to learn about medicine in that way, but it is extremely unlikely to produce a good doctor. Doctors need patients. They are learning all the time as they deal with and treat different patients for similar diseases. There is no easy sub-stitute for clinical experience. That means taking each case and trying to build up a body of expertise, and medical and per-sonal knowledge and wisdom. When doctors are taught, specific cases are used as examples. Trainee doctors examine patients with interesting and ordinary problems to become good doctors. In trying to teach medical ethics to busy, practical-minded doctors, the case study method is widely used.

In the past, the philosophy and ethics of medicine was sufficiently taught by osmosis. Just being with senior doctors was meant to guarantee that a junior doctor learned how to behave properly and to relate to patients in a professional manner. One of the problems with this approach was that medical students learned bad as well as good habits. As students are taught clinical skills by practice, so they are increasingly being taught ethical and person skills in the same kind of way. This is no guarantee that good, ethically correct doctors will result, but it is far better than the old way or no ethical teaching at all.

We began the book by arguing that the nature of the relationship between a doctor and patient was a partnership. This partnership is one between people. For it to work well, both people have to give themselves to it and take responsibility to make the partnership function properly. Given the skill, training, expertise and power of the doctor in the relationship, the doctor must take a greater responsibility for the patient partner and his or her medical care and well-being. For this to happen doctors must not just be good doctors. They must also be good.

For many years, medical schools selected students who were brilliant at the scientific subjects, which are so important for the practice of medicine. There was an unfortunate tendency to forget the person and social skills necessary to make a good doctor. Regrettably, society ended up with a generation which was scientifically brilliant in the medical field, but often was not very good with patients. Some doctors lack the personal skills to relate well and easily with patients and to inspire trust and confidence. The selection process and the nature of medical education have now tried to correct this flawed concentration on academic and scientific ability, and give much more weight to people skills. Part of this is to ask what really makes a good doctor and what are the virtues of good medical practice.

The history of the practice of medicine has been of generations of selfless women and men, who have sacrificed themselves for the benefit of their patients. Such qualities as genuine love for humanity and a commitment to the care and well-being of others are vital if doctors are to fulfil their role towards patients and society, and if patients are to trust themselves and their health to the medical profession. While doctors are all too human and will make mistakes both clinically and morally, society must support them and encourage them to maintain the highest standards in medicine and ethics.

Notes on Chapter 12
1. Declaration of Geneva 1968; Declaration of Helsinki 1975.
2. Beauchamp and Childress, *Principles in Biomedical Ethics* (OUP, Oxford, 1983).
3. *Regina* v. *Cox*, Winchester Crown Court (September 1992).

INDEX